The Light Side
Of The Oneness

By
Margaret Rogers Van Coops
Prof. Ph.D DCH(IM)

Copyright 2020 Prof. Margaret Rogers Van Coops. All rights reserved

Cover design by Margaret Roges Van Coops and Katie Kamara

Sumaris Center
321 Farallon Dr.,
Lake Havasu City. AZ 86403
USA

profmargaretrvc@gmail.com
drmargaretrvc@gmail.com
http://www.sumariscenter.com

No part of this book may be reproduced, stored in a retrieval system, or transmitted by any means without the written permission of the author

Published by Soma Fusion Media LLC in collaboration with Sumaris Enterprises 2020

ISBN: 978-1-63625-575-0 (Digital)
       978-1-63625-591-0 (Print)

Because of the dynamic nature of the internet, any web addresses or links contained in this book may have changed since publication and may no longer be valid. The view expressed in this work are solely those of the author and do not necessarily reflect the views of the publisher.

Table Of Contents

All of Prof/Dr. Margaret's books are available as e-books from
her website and/or www.somafusionmedia.com
and on wwww.amazon.com.

INTRODUCTION
The Oneness Has Our Heart, Mind, Body, & Spirit In Unity With All That Is!

When you think of God, pray, and ask for help, most of you want to believe that your prayers are heard. However, there is always the *Doubting Thomas* within all of us. How can we know with certainty that what we think, feel and share, is actually being transmitted into the vastness of space, as we look up at the sky and hope!

The reality of The Oneness is that it is not space, or the planets that float about in many patterns within the Cosmos. It is in reality, purely energy that has taken form in many dynamic ways that are beyond our comprehension. When we think of energy, we identify it with our own bodies, how they feel and whether or not we are active or passive. In each case our measures of energy are always physical in nature. This Earth, our Planet is ideal for life, and is the most amazing place where all aspects of life can thrive, provided there is harmony in the way all species survive. At this time of writing, in my honest opinion, I see that we have forgotten this rule during the emergence and experiences of living in The Piscean Age.

If we go back in time, we can discover from ancient artifacts that there was once times of other Ages in the past, that in many ways, are mysterious to our ways of thinking today. Those Ages were astrological times when this world was transforming. It is now known that we can recognize how the Sun Signs of Aries, Taurus, Gemini, Cancer, Leo, Virgo, Libra, Scorpio, Sagittarius, Capricorn, Aquarius, and Pisces created influences that occurred in their individual cycles.

Each Universal Sun-sign cycle lasted approximately over 2,652 years, providing periods of Spiritual Growth in varieties of ways. What occurred throughout the final influence of the last Sun Sign, we call The Piscean Age, was destruction. It should be noted here that many of the Ages past, as we call them today, are actually a part of the complete cycle of The Great Piscean Age that lasted for over 31,824 years.

Pisces is considered by us to be the final lesson. The end of one cycle and the beginning of a new one. However, to understand the inner workings of Astrology, one must know that while the Great Ages are entered in a clockwise circle, the inner Ages of the Sun-signs flow in a anti-clockwise direction. The existence of this way of understanding the past is the first lesson in knowing about friction. In the overview The Great Age of Pisces was a period of perception and trial and tribulations. As an ending symbol, it is the end of survival by chance, along with many ways and means to learn the hard way, what not to do! We have spent over 31,000 plus years, struggling to live in ways that will ultimately lead to unity!

In 2008 we entered the overlap of the Great Piscean Age into The Great Aquarian Age. What followed is the results you see today! People are in discord, full of animosity, with heated battles over what is needed to be continued, versus an acceptance of change. This battle of losing the past, versus gaining the future in better formats, has been actively a trying issue for every country. Wars have sparked destruction, lack of support, food, help and so much more that is a part of The Dark Side of our nature. We who are light workers, must understand The Dark Side of our nature and so, I respectfully request you read my book, The Dark Side first, before going on with this book. It is essential for all of us to understand that we are being stripped of the old ways and are now being encouraged to create and embrace new ways for all life forms. Each is to listen, learn, and heal before trying to make something new that works productively for us all, which will be given by The Oneness.

Going back in time, during the overlap of The Aries Age, with The Great Piscean Age, which lasted for over two and a half thousand years, under the rule of Archangel Michael, we have fought over land issues relative to belongings and trade. No matter how much anyone wanted peace, the opposite was achieved, born out of pain and suffering. We learned to control, manipulate, and even kill for the sake of a trinket. No one felt safe. Nations were victims of the victorious. The aspect of God's influence was in the physical creation of an awakened desire for learning. This Aries cycle stimulated desires and acts without thought, causing many to conquer and kill in the name of a leader. Each violent lesson set us on a pathway of destruction and annihilation. The Aries Age was one or torment, slavery, exploration, and stimulations in understanding the nations of the world, since voyagers explored the oceans, making this world a little smaller in our minds. Cities were annihilated, since the Earth was actively cleansing and shifted its axis, and ultimately many species died.

The Taurus Age was much more physical, in that people wanted the finer things in life. This was a period in history when stubbornness reared its head in the forms of creative inventions. The Egyptian and Romans along with the Greeks were the powers of the day. Philosophy and religious beliefs were important. Seers and spiritual ways were the norm for all. Yes, somehow, they were influenced by the trades, the foreigners who visited and yes unusual encounters with other species from other places in the Universe. These combined influences awakened the need for understanding, and learning was popular around the world. Everyone was fighting for changes in life standards, though trade included slavery, still exists. In this period great buildings were formed for all the world to see. Show and tell was highly important when it came to trade. Organization was imperative if armies were to receive rations, tools of war and much more, which often fell short causing armies to rebel against the Roman Empire. This Sun Cycle period of earthly Taurus was consistently both creative and destructive.

The Gemini Cycle began as an Age in 2001 as we celebrated the turn of the Millennium. People gathered together in joy, celebrating hope and expectations of a better century. Glimpse of what might be, began to appear as individuals created new ways and means to travel, communicate and to evolve all our species. The internet was the prime tool to connect us all, along with frequent flights to visit relatives, or do business, as well as, to travel to far off exotic places, there to buy homes and escape the toils of work. Life seemed good. But, what occurred with the world economy was a downward slop to the destruction of what was. Unknown to many, we had entered the Sun Cycle Age of Gemini and the end of The Great Age of Piscean history. The question in everyone's mind was, "Who will be the new leader to save us all from annihilation?" So under the influence of this ancient Piscean Age of ending what was, more wars broke out, bombing and strife, etc. A summation of all the thousands of Piscean years were exposed within the following years. We killed, maimed, wounded, destroyed homes and businesses world-wide. We fought over money, battled for cheap prices, the freedom of women, and even argued over simple issues.

At the same time, all the far distant planets moved closer bringing us a warning. Prepare for change or lose all that you have. Instead people ignored this warning, putting hours into communications on telephones, tablets, computers and in travel. Money was spent foolishly. Enter the Corona Virus and the physical break we all needed.

There have been great Sages of the past who had, in visions, seen how this New Great Age Of Aquarius would begin under the influence of the Sun Cycle Age of Gemini. Gemini offers us two points of view! Can we be integrated and expressive, while listening and learning new ways to behave and to work. Or, must we be revolutionists who argue, fight for a useless cause or a new plan that changes with time, energy, and money? This Age of Gemini will last for approximately 2,622 years. We have just stepped into this Age of Gemini in 2008, leaving The Great Piscean Age behind. However, even though everyone referred to 'The Shift' at that time, none seemed to realize how the Age of Gemini was manifesting on a daily basis. Individuals are now becoming aware that there are always two sides to every situation, and every way must be searched thoroughly if we are to choose the right pathway, where all peoples of this world are at peace, fed, clothed, working and contributing to The Human race as equals. No, this will not happen tomorrow, but it will eventually, by the time this Age of Gemini ends, according to Archangel Haniel.

Each Archangel has their turn in each regeneration that occurs within us. Archangel Haniel is the primary leader in The Gemini Age, supported by the other six Archangels. During the whole of the Piscean Age, all Archangels shared their influences with individuals. Raphael was the original lead in supporting and developing humans into a survival mode, while Gabriel stimulated Human existence to listen to The Oneness, known as God, through the birth of new religions and philosophy. Archangel Michael was to teach us the power of self in existence while encouraging friction and growth through negativity that led towards awareness of balance and harmony in finding the positive traits of human kind. Archangel Michael then brought us an understanding of inner peace, divine love and wisdom through discord and assimilation of what had gone before in The Ages past. Haniel now has the tough task of teaching us how to unify and trust our leaders who will transform the way we live and share in this life, over the next 2000 or more years. The other Archangels are supporting him in his leadership. See my book: *Journey Into an Unknown World; The Way To Oneness Revisited* that he and other Great Ascended Master Spirits channeled through me back in 1986.

The Archangels all have a say in the way we learn. Below is a list of their abilities to teach us wisely, extracted from the book mentioned above.

Rachael: His Archetype is a King: The way of the King is to use the wisdom of the collective Soul. In form he takes the lead, using inborn knowledge and power to lead the way.

Michael: His Archetype is a Warrior: The way of the Warrior is one of instinct. In form he uses his natural drive with desire to challenge and explore, and in so doing, leads the way.

Gabriel: His Archetype is the Priest: The way of the Priest is to manifest The Creator. In form he serves Mankind with high ideals of other worldly consciousness as a leader.

Barakiel: His Archetype is a Slave: The way of the Slave is to inspire the expression of The Creator. In form he serves Mankind in a supportive interactive role which leads the way towards spiritual growth.

Haniel: His Archetype is a Sage: The way of the Sage is to express innate wisdom. In form he shows Mankind his good judgment and shrewd abilities in practical Divine Expression and leads the way.

Phaniel: His Archetype is an Artisan: The way of the Artisan is to express emotions. In form the Artisan reminds others, by his creative expression, of all that they are in The Oneness. In this way he leads.

Zaphiel: His Archetype is a Scholar: The way of the Scholar is to see all things as transcendental. In form he serves the other Archetypes by observing their actions and being available as a go-between. He accepts change and welcomes it, thus leading the way.

Since we are constantly supported by the Archangels who have given us freedom of expression, we may make mistakes and learn the hard way, but we are also directed by them, to find our inner truth and to develop our personality and character, that is encoded into our DNA long before we incarnated now.

Our Spirit is encoded with the reasons we have incarnated, the things we want to do with our talents and skills as well as to follow in the footsteps of our ancestors. We are equally encoded with the ability to absorb our lesson not only form those we encounter, but also from our Spirit Guides, Ascended Masters and the higher echelon that provide us with insights, inspiration, and a sense of purpose.

FORWARD
The Oneness Is Not A Place.

The Oneness was formed out of the Ethers of energy called The Dark Side! Friction formed gases, liquids, and solids. Violent eruptions formed structures out of which came lasting forms. Forms were destroyed, time and time, again until consciousness was developed. Then came a great awakening.

In my book, *Quantum Entanglement: A Paranormal Point Of View,* you can learn more about the energy of The Oneness. Here, I wish to point out that it is nigh on impossible for us to understand the vastness of The Oneness and all that lies within it. As we look out at the Cosmos and realize now, that somewhere out there is another planet with life on it, we still are unable to know what that planet is like. This leaves us with imagination.

Imagination is the core of our perceptions. It is released by passion where desire motivates us to try and achieve some form of creation. You could be wanting a fence, and have no idea how to build one, but with due diligence, asking those who do know, and making sure you learn from them, you will build that fence. However, there are those of us who are pioneers in creativity, and their ways are likely to be completely different from what has been done before. In observation, others may be looking in admiration, while still others will be determined to pick the work to pieces with critiques that are usually arising from a fear of dealing with something new. The truth is that we are all afraid of change.

Change is the core seat of power in dealing with the unknown. The unknown about God, Angels, and the like, even demons, is for us, of paramount importance to all that is unknown. It is essential that we all awaken to the choices we have to make when dealing with a new situation. As we embrace new ideas, new experiences and eventually overcome fear, we move into aggression that often houses negative anger. Anger then becomes the passion that stimulates us to resist, but ultimately, to want to know more. Then curiosity arises, giving form to learning. In this way, over eons of time, we experiment with new events. As new events transform and become orderly, then habit and routines occur. As those habitual things take over, we each become slothful, safely ensconced within routines that become boring. As time passes, dissatisfaction arises causing many to blame and shame others for living within their circumstances. Only then, do people look to others to be rescued, and if not saved, become party to riots that occur.

We have entered The Great Aquarian Age with a fully loaded baggage of out of date history, that no longer service us. We blame our politicians, Kings, Presidents, and other leaders for our bad economy, no health support, and little food to eat. Yet, each of us has, at some time, felt guilt about not doing your fair share of the work. Work is not just toiling at a job! It is coming up with new ideas to adapt and learn and evolve into a new state of being. If everyone could just stop and see themselves, like watching a movie of self, then an awareness of the form you take, how you walk, talk and postulate would be revealed to you. Of course, this rarely happens since most are busy critiquing appearances from a beauty point of view.

We are all beautiful within our soul's perception which shines out within the Spirit Body of self that resides in your body. The problem is not what you know, but what you do not know! Every experience you have is a lesson in discovering more about who you are. Day by day you have thousands of emotional, mental, physical, spiritual experiences that often go un-noticed by your conscious mind and heart. However, your Spirit never forgets.

With the lock-down caused by the Corona Virus, which in itself is an amazing organism, with a nucleus that has twenty amino acids within its proteins, so that it can adapt in seconds. It has taught each one of us to know that we have discovered just how boring life is without action. We humans have, in our own way, adapted with only twelve amino acids, needing to take in vegetation and foods from animals that provide us with all the regeneration and healing we need. In this wholesome way, we have become the most advanced species in our world. Surely, this is now a time of reduction, when we each learn to look inwards for beautiful answers in how to improve our world, the way we use it, and what we do while living on it.

I sincerely hope that, what you are about to read, channeled from The Archangels for me to share with you, will intrigue you and draw you in to receive all that is already waiting to be given to you as you surrender to your destiny. Then you will fully appreciate how wonderful you and this world are together and, just how amazingly spiritual and joyful you feel, once you connect with The Oneness and all it has to offer.

CHAPTER ONE
In The Beginning Was The Oneness & The Oneness Was All That Is.

Far beyond any concept of time and space was a source of energy that had been sentient within its existence. Energy abounded in and around itself. In time that energy became too violent and aggressive. It needed to expand and without knowing it, continued to generate more and more energy until it impacted and was separated into two parts. One part was naive and fearful of the change, while the other looked back at its other half, and then, began to generate sounds of friction, repeating what had happened before and so it divided again and again. The original Fragment was watching and absorbing all the experiences the other Fragment had created. They drifted far apart, and each had within it a knowing where it had come from. Over eons of time, each Fragment would, in honor of their memories, create something new out of the ethers of energy they had created and managed until a desire for form was manifested.

Early forms were chaotic and disorganized, each fragment having forgotten their role and purpose in exploration. They were beginning to dissolve and disappear. The original Fragment was concerned and drew them back into Its side and rejuvenated them and bid them go once again and explore. There was a difference this time! They had a knowing, a remembrance of where they had been and what they had done, and in fear of losing their way, asked for direction. They were given memory in images to reacquaint themselves with all forms they had made, and they too saw the chaos and were sorely afraid they would make the same errors. And so it was that the Higher Arche of The Oneness was born. A group of wiser Fragments decided to make themselves into forms and to experiment. In eons of time, they learned a great deal about unity and purpose versus disorder and separation.

As the Fragments marvel at themselves, they began to create other forms which, in time, also became chaotic. It was within this era long forgotten, that the now original Prime Fragment had grown larger and larger with the absorption of all other Fragment's experiences that had been shared with it. It was overwhelmed with emotions and fast losing control of itself. This Prime Fragment, you call God, pondered long, and in time, realized that if it was to survive, it must balance the polarities of action versus inaction, mistakes versus successes, understanding versus ignorance and the list went on and on until The Prime Fragment was overwhelmed with its awakening sense of a need for order.

Since The Prime Fragment was busy holding all experiences, it needed to delegate the responsibility of feedback to itself! It needed Delegates that were both creative and loyal. Many Fragments volunteered to create the first Plane of Evolution with seven Levels within it, each section overseeing all happenings. And so it was, that a Collective Soul Group of Fragments were united in one common goal. To keep the balance and the experiences ever evolving in harmony with The Prime Fragment, now seen as the 'All knowing Fragment,' whose energy was so expanded that it was beyond measure.

The Soul Group of Fragments named themselves The Universal Brotherhood of Descension, they being in charge of the control of fragmentation that was continually repeated into millions of fragments, all coming and going with no purpose, beyond to exist and sub-divide. They had to have a plan that would work for all time. Something so strong and so sacred to all involved that all would obey the rules in any circumstance. But, they needed a base structure to build upon! There was much consideration given to the purpose of existence which, in time, became a leading question. So many Fragments had created so many forms, which you could call shapes, animation, expression and yes, consciousness which led to purpose. Since so many fragments had many different purposes, it became obvious that there needed to be control between both those who were far away from the hub of light where energy was over-active, to Fragments who were considered lost from the whole with no feedback to The Prime Fragment who felt an emptiness pervading it form.

Thus, we were in agreement to become The Primary Leading Soul Group who in turn created the first original collective Soul Group that amalgamated and unified themselves to become individual Spirits in various created physical forms. They were to experience many different kinds of forms. We all united in creating gas into liquids, and liquids into solids, and solids into worlds with many forms, and all were well pleased. All that they had created was encoded with each of their treasures of experiences and successes in reconnecting with all of the lower lost fragments that had travel far and wide, in their quest for a place to call home. This new coding was primal and balanced in that both parts needed one another. In time it was called The Dark and The Light. Every Fragment was encoded with both. Each had a code within that ensure a journey of discovery with a return to The Prime Soul Group, who in turn fed that information back to The Prime Fragment and so it was that consciousness and awareness was transmitted from The Prime Fragment down to all forms of existence and all forms of existence returned for rejuvenation and the sharing.

In your time, this Prime Fragment became your God and the Prime Soul Group became your stimulators, instigators, inventors and most importantly, the creators of Divine Love and Divine Wisdom that was shared throughout The Oneness. And so it was appearing to be the paradise of balance in The Prime Fragment. Then something changed! Fragments began to take various forms in living creatures on various planets. They transformed energy at every whim, never staying in the same shape for long. The Prime Soul Group was rejected and those who took forms were feeling God-like and discounted their connections with The Prime Fragment. This was truly the beginning of choice in separation. The Prime Fragment was swamped with emotions from those experiencing forms. Negative emotions were fast destroying the balance of The Oneness and the Soul Prime Group made a choice too!

From this time on, Fragments were allowed free space, will, and experiences to explore and create. There was one condition! Each fragment must return to the fold of The Oneness to share experiences and recover from the long separation that had almost annihilated the memory of The Oneness.

From that time on, the Prime Directive from The Prime Fragment was to follow these rules, no matter where any Fragment found itself. If it should not do so, then it would be allowed to stay far away, and to struggle with the problems of their own making until they wished to return and share. It was made clear that no fragment shall be cast out or lost, and so it was that each Fragment had a homing signal within their consciousness in the form of Divine Love and Wisdom, that would lie dormant, until truly needed, in order to cease their chaos and return to the balance of all that The Oneness had to offer.

By this time, many forms were ascending back to the heart of The Oneness, while a few sought new things elsewhere. It was during this time that more Soul Groups of fragments were created. Each Soul Group had a focus. That focus was, and is today, to ensure the safety of all Fragments while away from the hub of The Oneness. As Fragments explore new ways and means of creation, they return and share their experiences, and as time passes they, in turn, prepare new cycles of learning for those who will leave, time and time again, on a mission to balance the worlds that have been created and all life on them.

Over Eons of Ages, long before Earth existed, separation and unity of Fragments continued. The Oneness has never stopped expanding, since each Fragment still creates a new fragment in separation of self. On your planet, the birth of a child brings the sharing and separation of each parent into the child's life as it grows. A big change occurs in both Mother and Father as they unite in love and welcome a child who will, in many ways, be just like them. Human form is truly the ultimate form in which to experience life in all its manifested ways.

We, The Archangels are the watchers who observe and balance both The Light and Dark Sides of each one of you. We also keep the flow of Fragments who exit and return in balance. We will never allow anyone to be lost. We know at all times where everyone is. We also understand that you have no sense of how our abilities radiate from us. Nor do you know how much we love each one of you. Love Divine knows no boundaries. Divine Wisdom understands all matters and, therefore, we always have answers when we are consulted for help.

Our memories of all the forms we have taken before The Primal Soul Council was formed, is never forgotten. Our abilities to know millions of conversations and reply instantly, with energy that is radiated to you, is the way of our source of life. We allow you to interpret your inner feelings and to understand the simplistic answer to your doubt. Trust, do, enjoy, and learn! These are your Human lessons. We will always walk beside you and steer you to the next cycle of your life. You are never alone!

Our roles in Ascension are unique and vitally important to the creation and existence of all that is active and passive. The active part of The Oneness is constantly receiving new input from your world, where your experiments in expansion and resistance stimulates us to provide further support. We inspire you with new ideas and emotional stimulation to learn more. Some Fragments are passive counter-balancers who remain in calm balance, providing an anchor that ensures some form of harmony. Those within The Primary Soul Group are able to constantly adapt and return advice and support to all Fragments that survive in far off places, as well as your own planet. It has become a priority for all aspects of existence to be integrated and absorbed into The Oneness, allowing it to expand and contract relative to the changes that occur consistently. We The Archangels are an important link between your world and others that are integrated at this time.

It should be understood that we and many other angelic beings are constantly active in inspiring and nurturing individual Fragments who are incarnated on many planets, most unknown to your species. The result of seclusion is to ensure the stability and unity within The Oneness, thus preventing chaos once again from destruction and annihilation.

Over eons of time, we began to organize more Soul Groups who would enter into physical form as leaders who would bring insightful information into form. The result was considered to be an experiment that led to a greater awakening of our role in becoming an active part of the Creator or as we explained earlier, The Prime Soul that absorbs all experiences shared throughout The Oneness. This primary role can only be described in your world as 'The All Knowing.' This state of Divine Wisdom was, and still is, the main stimuli for all to endear and support the original form, that is now long transformed and charged with Divine Presence of Love and Wisdom in all species, providing tender care and support.

As we support each Fragment that choses to become a Human, we never fail to support them, even when they are lost in negativity and illusions. However, we cannot invade or interfere in the freedom of each Fragment to explore, discover, and merge with the newness of existences in a variety of ways. We advise, support, and bring lessons of truth when asked to show the way.

Your world is changing its form and with it all who live within Earth's vibration. This is a time to free yourself from the bondage of fear, pain, anger, and guilt, while accepting loss as a sign of change. Move forward and embrace this change. Give of yourself, your time, experiences, and inventions, to those seeking help to assist the younger ones in a variety of ways to speed this change, embracing peace over the next two hundred years. The pattern of The Oneness is now embellishing the need to return in Ascension with awareness to return to The Prime Soul Group for new ways and means to achieve serenity, love and appreciation for all who unite in peace, while assisting those who flounder on a daily basis.

CHAPTER TWO
In The Beginning Is The Ending

Long ago the words of your bible were given to the peoples of the world to understand self and purpose. Since our basic need to expand our forms was our priority, it was easy to create masses out of gases and liquids. Many Universes were created and in each case, they were given the Soul Structure Coding, which is still the finite necessity for any form in existence where life is animated.

The seven days of Creation were in fact seven Ages of experimentation in making worlds and giving them life in a variety of ways. Since energy can be manipulated, it was proven that extremes in friction could be defined as dense and dark or expansively flexible within the light of The Oneness of all that is! It is our intention in this book to take you into the expansive light, which will allow you to glimpse and contemplate the value of each single life lived on Earth, and those who support an incarnated Spirit and those Fragments who may never incarnate.

To understand the light, one must know how it is created. When friction occurs as a result of gasses exploding, new forms manifest in liquid, that when cooled over eons of time, formed planets, and a variety of other forms that are not known to you while you live on Earth. But, the good news is, that you do have a deep-seated sense of belonging in The Oneness that reminds you to return to it. Here, we wish to share that The Oneness includes all forms, planets and a great deal of strange things that are not yet revealed to you. By having various states of amnesia, it protects you from taking the wrong pathway in your life.

Each one of you is encoded with a Soul connection to The Oneness via your Soul Group. A Soul Group can consist of hundreds of thousands of Fragments who are all unique, being differently encoded and exceedingly adaptable to change. When a great need of change arises on your planet, a unification of desire pushes each to find a solution. Planet Earth has a unique opportunity to adapt and change frequently, unlike other planets not in your solar system. This is not to say that other planets are not in discord, but rather to say that they are life forces in different forms, that have a different purpose. Those planets will never be a part of your world in any way.

With regard to Alien encounters on your planet, we concede there were many. Over eons of ages, your species have evolved as alien interventions succeeded and failed. This interaction of aliens has karmically entwined all species that lived on your planet. The growth and spiritual awareness of Ascension has dynamically changed your approach to form and life. Since The Oneness allows complete freedom of choice and adventure, it has brought other species to you to embellish your forms and your perceptions of life and spirituality. You are all, in fact, aliens! You are highly developed in your planetary coding to seek better ways of survival and of awakening to the voice of The Oneness, who will lead you towards unity and peace.

From your earthly point of view, your beginnings were created by God. Your world is evolving beyond that belief. Science has begun to evolve in your consciousness. You have learned to create terrible weapons of destruction, to kill and maim for no reason beyond primal thinking. You have learned the hard way that peace lies in unity and love for all. Now comes the hard time to entwine your skills and talents in new ways that will be once again a New Beginning, when together you will build a world of unity and peace. As each rises to the understanding of unity, so your world, as you know it, will change. Every step you each take will be important to the change; however small your part is to play. You are no less or more important than another.

Together you will unite and recreate this planet in ways yet not understood.

With the new development in technology, science and bio-chemistry, you will discover that health issues are easily controlled and, in time, to know how to regenerate tissue, arms, legs, etc., to regrow following an accident. This may sound exciting, but it comes at a price! More controversy, arguments in disbeliefs and philosophy. Where new ideas flow, there is always resistance to change. You can expect a great deal of trauma as time passes until peace is recognized and unity is established. By then you will be a new species reborn and your goals will take on a new dimension that is not revealed now.

Having spoken about the beginning, let us now address the ending! Each species that is alive on Earth, must ultimately die. You may ask why? The truth is that without each individual being returning to The Oneness, there would be no friction, and the end result would be nothing in existence. When individual beings return to The Oneness, they return with experiences that are considered by us, a challenge. Life on Earth brings a constant lesson of Dark versus Light back into The Oneness, which temporarily upsets our balance. What follows is our own needs to adapt too. When we find that balance, we are then able to be calm and embrace those who return, once again embracing all that is shared without issues. As we merge, we bring new ideas, hopes and dreams into form for a new beginning.

Within The Oneness are many new beginnings, some small and other ginormous, since it involves a shift in the whole of The Oneness. In such a case, we all shift and adapt to new ways to express ourselves individually and collectively, as smaller units of Fragments take the lead with trials and tribulations that once again generate friction. By now, you have come to understand that friction is the fuel for life. Life depends on both the heat and the cold. The Dark and the Light both contain dark and light forces of energy that are in a never-ending cycle of friction which always results in adaptive growth of form and spiritual awakening.

A beginning can be a change in perception, leading to an emotional explosion of energy, stimulated by rage or love. Passion must be active and sometimes overwhelming in order for changes to occur. It is no different in The Oneness. When millions of people die on Earth, we are busy helping those Spirits to leave their bodies and to awaken to The Oneness. As they recall all that they are, they are brought back into the Light of The Oneness. Those that linger in the Dark, will continue to fight for a cause, purpose and, in time, an awakening.

In order for you to understand our world we must use your imagination, intelligence, and emotions to explore our world. As you know when you die you return to what we call The Astral, which you may call Heaven. There you will explore the importance of your last life, focusing on what you have learned and how it integrates with Past Lives. You will also perceive how your Soul Structure Coding has aided you to achieve success, as well as, to recall the results of your efforts and experiences in clinging to your own purpose. That physical purpose would have had both negative and positive emotional attachments.

When you have assimilated the information, it is passed into The Oneness to be shared with everyone. Everything that you share has an importance to The Oneness as a whole. Your feedback and your experiences are then accepted as an important part of integration. Whether you have been a bad or good person on Earth is not important. What is important is what your life's experiences have done to cause changes in expression and love. Your life, whether inventive or in acceptance, has influenced many other incarnated Fragments who will, in turn, react or respond to those things you have done, leaving a strong impression on those left behind. In this way, your life has been important. One might ask how a person living in acceptance without action can impress those left behind. The answer is simple! Your life lived has in some way stimulated others to find alternative ways to exist. On Earth, there are many who spend a great deal of time affecting others without even knowing it.

Likewise, those who are Ascended Masters, Spirit Guides, and Earthbound Spirits, who have interacted with you subliminally while you were alive, are also affected by you and the circumstances you have needed help with. By working with these ascended ones, each person receives guidance in dreams, or in trance modes, such as meditation or day-dreaming, Whatever you have experienced is then shared throughout The Oneness in preparation for when you will return to the fold. Upon arrival, there is a celebration of your life, acceptance of all that you have done, whether good or bad, since there is no judgment in our world of unity.

Once you have harmonized self with your previous lives and become aware of your need to return and reincarnate, The Oneness will stimulate you to prepare for your return. Plans will begin, relative to the new plans of evolvement for the Ascension of awareness on Earth. Spirits prepare for their lives to come in The Astral, some waiting as much as hundreds of years, or more, to manifest a new life in your future or the future of your grandchildren. When you look back on Earth through recorded history, you can easily see how various individuals have, by their actions, created a wave of consciousness to accept change.

As we write this book, we wish to remind you that you are collectively encoded with all other Humans sharing a *Goal of Spiritual Growth*. Yes, The Oneness is encoded with all aspects of all entwined parts of The *Infinite Soul Structure Coding*. Thus the manifestation of new forms always continues. Your world is changing and so is each one of you as you incarnate with a new *Soul Structure Coding,* that has been carefully planned, long before you incarnated. You have already bonded with thousands of Fragments who will enter into your life as you evolve, and many with others in The Oneness who will guide and direct you along your pathway. As you age, you will awaken to the deeper wisdom that lies within. During your later years you will transform your life towards leaving something of value to the newly born who are programmed to take your world to the next level of growth.

In like manner, we who salute you in living a life, thank you for the physical experiences that we no longer have or need to have, but which keeps us active in assisting The Oneness to continue its growth. Our work is to balance all that is in discord, while stimulating all that is in harmony, to flow throughout the Cosmos and back into the Oneness. In this way we evolve constantly.

There are many Planes of Evolution. Within each Plane are Levels of unexpected growth, on our part, as we struggle to keep the balance. Some of the Planes are in darkness, while others are in extreme light. In each Plane are Seven Levels of spiritual growth for all. As the darkness fades, new forms are created that will in some way evolve differently from those who have gone before. In like manner, you who are evolving Fragments (Spirits in form) will adapt and change from life to life and when in The Oneness, evolve from Level to Level in spiritual awareness.

While you may remember the birthing of your life, you may not remember where you came from. Each encoded Spirit is the form a Soul must take to incarnate. The Spirit of each is encoded with a Soul Structure Coding, Ancestor's DNA and, while living, to absorb RNA from family, friends, enemies, and the creatures of the Earth. Unknown to an incarnated Spirit, now a Human, are all their ancestors who will assist spiritually in his/her life as it evolves. The common thread of the lesson left by ancestors must continue throughout each generation and frequently for generations to come. In this way, once again, energy is shifting back and forth between the negative and positives states of existence on Earth.

You can now understand the importance of your life, however meek, humble, or combatant and rough! What you do on a daily basis affects others, who in turn share or react, passing on the lesson of growth to all who become involved. Growth must not only be on a daily basis while living on Earth, but also an active part of The Oneness, by providing energy through action that awakens meaning and purpose for all. By using your creative talents in expressive ways, you leave a message of importance for others to learn. Whether you write a book, act in a play, or run a marathon, someone is influenced by what you do and likely, will become a follower and, in time, bring forth something of value for self, the world, and the Oneness.

In final analysis, each person has a job to do. That job is to stir up those they meet to become active in some way, which in turn, develops a consciousness in developing ways and means to experience Earth in new ways. Hence, the creative mind develops new items of comfort, growth, and stability, that results in lessons to be learned. If you look back over the past two thousand years, you see a time when many could not read or write. Today in your world, everyone is given education and experiences through what is called The Internet.

In finalizing this chapter, let us use your imagination of how the Internet is expanding your awareness and consciousness. You can now watch and look at images from far off places. Places, in past times, where you would never visit; people you would never physically meet; lessons you would never have had. Today, there is nothing denying you the opportunity to learn and most importantly, to understand a great deal of information that would likely, in previous lives, have passed over your head, unless you suddenly felt inspired to search. Never before has each Fragment had the opportunity to itemize and explore so much.

In The Oneness all aspects of life are felt immediately, understood vicariously, and lived emotionally through the lives of Fragments that are incarnated. We Ascended Ones, salute you for your courage and support in helping us to keep The Oneness from falling apart. As you adapt physically, we adapt spiritually. When we combine our efforts, we bring an awakening not only to your world, but to ours. In this united pattern of beginning and ending, we all evolve in Ascension, ultimately feeding back to the Prime Fragment, that amalgamates all aspects of form into a knowing of its existence in many forms, all of which are in diversity of the ways and means of continued existence.

Since life on Earth is complicated, it is often believed that The Oneness is complicated too. The truth is that all aspects of The Oneness are constantly being upgraded to suit the changes that occur while Fragments are in separation. Since Fragments come and go in seconds, there is always a lot to do for us to balance and harmonize The Oneness. We each know our place and do the necessary work to keep the Universal energy of all that is, united.

Should a Fragment fall into despair and the Darkness, we will go and find them, draw them into the first light to remind them of the source of Light and their place in it. Because there is no time in The Oneness, those who linger in the darkness have no sense of how long they have been lost. They simply reminisce their past life until they are bored and blocked from spiritual growth. At that time, we arrive to help them to ascend back into The Astral, and there to heal their suffering. As we said earlier, no one fragment is every forgotten or lost.

So what is in The Dark Matter? Imagine if you will you are wondering in a dark cave and cannot see anything, or that you are blind. You would quite naturally feel your way around and listen intently for something to make a sound. In time, if you could hear nothing and in finding nothing, you would begin to feel depressed and alone. Perhaps you would use your imagination and create a friend to talk to, or wallow in self-pity. Of course, there are many ways we learn to be negative on Earth, and those negative ideas, traits and feelings are carried by the Spirit, which darkens their Soul into believing negative spiritual thoughts. Hence the spirit feels cast out and alone.

Those lost Souls are brought back to The Oneness where they connect with those of a similar vibration. The Second Plane of Evolution is often filled with Lost Souls who take many strange forms, relative to their isolation and lack of Divine Love and Divine Wisdom. This in your imagination is 'The Devil's Domain' where evil exists. This Plane serves as an anchor for The Oneness, where a constant reminder of chaos is recalled and controlled, by helping these Fragment to transform into embracing the light of the Upper Planes.

For every beginning, there will always be an ending. In the ending is always a new beginning. The Oneness ensure this pattern continues for all time.

CHAPTER THREE
The Spirit World

We have spoken about the presence of the Plane of Elusion, often called the Second Plane of Ascension. There are in fact Seven Planes of Ascension. The First Plane is completely in darkness where all forms must struggle to survive. These are the babies of creation born out of chaos so long ago. They are able to procreate new forms and to survive in darkness in a world they feel is their own.

Within this First Plane of Creation, each Fragment must find its own way to knowing that there is more to discover and explore. As a Soul/Spirit baby has no form, it being pure energy, it must evolve to take up shape, and in so doing, acquire momentum. On the First Level of this Plane many newly created Fragments interact in awareness by bumping into one another, while exchanging energies in knowing that self exists. This is not unlike a newly conceived baby in the womb on Earth when the Soul becomes a Spirit embracing form in darkness within the womb. Here we see a Spirit subliminally reliving the acceptance of the Dark Side of one's nature, encoded within its *Soul Structure Coding,* that has been chosen long before embodiment. We must all be prepared to live up to the challenge of dealing with the Dark Side of life on Earth. Hence the need to remember the First Plane of Life and Evolution and subsequent Ascension through the Seven Levels leading to the First Level of The Second Plane of Evolution.

The Second Plane of Evolution provides an interesting twist to existence. Unlike the First Plane, where the emphasis is on just being in existence, this Second Plane is about self-discovery in various forms, actions, deeds, and general performance. This is the Kindergarten of our world where each new Soul must learn about its own existence and potential. Throughout the Seven Levels of this Plane, a Soul must learn to know its own power and, since it is still in the darkness, must learn to manipulate energy to suit its own purpose. Its desire for spiritual growth leads to it generating a new form, called a Spirit. If an Ascended Master enters this Plane of Evolution, there is a risk of contamination from the Dark Matter where forms are unstable and consciousness equally so. Nevertheless, this type of encounter leads to spiritual awakening in some Fragments, who seek insights and inspirations about themselves and their personal journey. Here bonding is learned and adhered to forever after. Passing though all Seven Levels on this Plane awakens the Fragment to a purpose. That purpose is to enter the Third Plane of Evolution.

The Third Plane of Evolution also has Seven Levels to pass through. Each Level provides an education about the existence of self and, the part that self has to play in acceptance of self as a Fragment Of The Oneness. By the time, the Fragment is on the Fifth Level of this Third Plane of Evolution, they have readily prepared to incarnate again and again, from the Sixth and Seventh Levels of this Plane of Evolution. Here it should be stated that the Fragment, now a Spirit, has been prepared for Its ascension into the imbalance of Earth's forms, ways and means. The Spirit of the Incarnated Soul has struggled and survived the two Lower Planes and is fully prepared for a simple life on Earth. They will incarnate back and forth between the Second and Third Planes until they find a form they wish to work with. It is important for you to realize that everyone has incarnated as animals, birds, various creatures, and early man. In this way human contact is tested in the young Spirit who is learning to survive, love and be loved. When you hold your pet in your arms, you may be holding a new Fragment who is experiencing your world and who will learn from you.

Some Humans are still incarnating back and forth from the Third Plane. They are often Fragments who have suffered a great deal in physical life and have returned to The Oneness in a very negative and destroyed state. They have been called Earthbound Spirits who have become evil. In truth they are broken Fragments; Souls who need a lot of counseling, healing, and love. Usually those who live in the Fifth Plane of Evolution will take on the role of healer and counselor, since they have evolved away from earthly happenings, but who are patient and endearing and able to transform those who are ready to enter the Forth Plane of Evolution. Fragments now ascending into Human form are bonded with Ascended Fragments in preparation for another life on Earth and a return to the Upper Astral eventually.

The Forth Plane of Evolution is a combination of the Planet Earth, The Lower Astral and Upper Astral Levels. This Forth Plane of Evolution is only conducive to the balance of light and dark, where the mixture of both aspects of creation must be sustained in order to keep the balance of The Oneness. When each Fragment incarnates as a Human, they will be exposed to all manner of dark and light events, where emotions are high, and fear paramount to the existence and continuation of life. With each life they live, there is always a need for cleansing and balancing when they return to the Astral after death.

Depending on the quality of life lived, and the negativity absorbed, the Spirit (Fragment), may return to the upper levels of the Second Plane of Evolution or the lower levels of the Third Plane of Evolution. Still later to return as a newly incarnated Spirit to the Forth Plane of Evolution, (Earth), in a life that will repeat a lost lesson. Yes, The Forth Plane of Evolution combines The Astral levels and Earth where lessons are repeated. If a positive life has led to great spiritual growth, then the Fragment will return to the Upper Astral, known as the Fifth Level, where many gather together to study and enter the spiritual Halls of

Learning.

This Forth Plane of Evolvement has a great deal to offer, since it is constantly transforming its size and shape, relative to the Oversoul presentations for a new Earth and a new cycle of growth. Each Fragment enters The Astral and incarnates with a new Soul Structure Coding, along with a new task to perform, time and time, again. Each incarnated Fragment has the freedom and intention to enlighten self, while developing talents and skills that will undoubtedly benefit Mankind. Thousands of lives can be lived by one Fragment over eons of time. So, we categorized spiritual growth in Fragments as infant, young, mature, old, ancient, Ascended Souls, Soul Groups, and The Prime Soul Group.

This is not to say that an Ascended Soul is better than any of the others, since we all learn at our own pace. While some may learn quickly, others may lag behind. Since there is no time in The Oneness, no one is counting the times one incarnates. However, here we must remind you of the Soul Groups who chose to incarnate at the same time, well prepared with an encoded point of reference. During your time now, we can see many who are encoded to assist your world to transform and become an awakened place of peace and harmony for a period of time. How the Collective Soul Groups who incarnated will act, is all relative to their individual Soul Structure Codings, their DNA & RNA, and the common factor of needs for change. This means that each has free will to express their needs and wants, while also coming together in some way, as a group, to make changes in many countries. Yes, many Old Souls have incarnated during this awakening of The Great Aquarian Age at its birth.

The Fifth Plane of Evolution is were those who have ascended enough times are no longer in need of surviving the perils of Earth. Instead they are the teachers who work diligently with those who return to the Lower and Upper Astral. Whether they teach in groups or one on one, the majority of students in the Astral will know what is being said, since by now, they are all telepathic and sensitive to energy changes that occur. You might say that everyone is very psychic, using their five senses rather than searching books and listening to tapes. However, in this Plane of Evolution, those things you see on Earth are also present in The Oneness. Your little house is there. Your pets are there. Everything you love surrounds you along with amazing healing energy from spiritual flowers, trees, and yes, water in an energetic form, where you bathe in energy, never getting wet.

The Sixth Plane of Evolution is a unique place where all things created, yet not manifested in form, are contemplated, and recorded. Here throughout the Seven Levels, work continues in creation to provide the tools, education, and inventions that will be shared with Ascended Masters, who will incarnate to give this source of new energy to the peoples of Earth. Some may never be known, since they work silently in closed rooms, leaving the world with a magical new toy, such as did Edison, when he brought Light to The World. The symbol was strong, but it took many centuries for it to be understood. Now you take light for granted and rarely value the importance of light until you lose it.

While this is not a class in understanding the whole of Ascension and Descension, it is important to understand that you have many tasks to perform for The Oneness, yourself, and others who follow you. The Fifth Plane of Evolution is full of all the beautiful things you can imagine, along with so many inventions yet to be shared on Earth. This plane is the physical energetic place of creation, though the energy is not of your world.

We spoke of friction earlier and must remind you that even on the Fifth Plane of Evolution, there is a need for a constant supply of energy exchange, that allows creation to occur. Those who dwell in this Plane are constantly absorbed into the ways of Earthly changes. Their experiences in knowing how to manipulate energetic states of evolvement, and to manage plans that will stimulate incarnating Fragments, long before they realize there is a need to return to Earth, is of Primal importance. Often, a Collective Soul Group has no idea what their part in the drama on Earth will be. Their strong sense of a connection with The Oneness leads them, through their Heart Chakras, to gather together, when the time comes, to stimulate the beginning of change. Each will have many individual plans and work towards success, while at the same time, subliminally following the signals of The Oneness that were set in motion long ago. Some aspects of creation, being millions of years old, are now firmly seeded in preparation for their latest incarnation, and the work they will collectively do to refresh Planet Earth once again

We must state clearly here that everyone living on Earth now, plus all those in the Astral as well as many Master Teachers are in sync with the Original Prime Quest; to follow a desire to transform the ways and means of life on Earth for the fifth time. There will be great changes in many ways over the next two hundred years. Be not afraid, for no one suffers without cause or purpose, in finding ways to awaken those who toil and lose their way. A collective group of people is a forceful energy. It will be necessary to master such energy in Unisom so that efforts will result in transformations for the better, yet to come.

CHAPTER FOUR
What is Light?

In your world, light has to be made. Various methods light your way. If you find yourself in pitch black darkness, as in the example of a cavern, your senses will grow confused and panic would surely follow. Panic will likely push you to accept death or to struggle, step by step until you feel air. Then with the sense of feeling, to follow the draft and in time to see a light. What a relief to know there is light!

In our world of The Oneness, there is no difference in our need to seek the light. Unlike you, we do not have physical senses unless we choose to manifest them into a Spirit form. Since we are not in form the way your bodies are densely built to live on Earth, it is vital for us to connect with you all in Spirit form. We are encoded and structured with spiritual energy just like you. As your body works, you dig into your desires and act upon them, causing your body to burn Dark Matter as fuel to re-energize you biochemically, while refueling with light absorbed from your Sun, or in learned disciplines of meditations. Relaxing with a warm electric light and a heater can be equally beneficial to you. There is only one difference between you and us! Your molecules are fixed in place, ours are flexible and constantly moving. Having such flexible molecules of light and dark allows us to transform our shape and also, to journey to distant places throughout the Cosmos, as you call it.

There are rules, however! No Fragment can go beyond its capability without another to assist. This unity in pairs, provides polarity in both monitoring and using both the dark and light energy, to manipulate form. The purpose and reason for this ability is to ensure that we each are capable of keeping the balance in any given circumstance.

Our abilities are far removed from earthly ways. We can speed across the heavens, change our forms to help someone. Move objects around and share information with others without having to visit them. These are simple things that you would understand. Those in the Astral will always practice control in how they manipulate energy. Sometimes mistakes are made, and lessons learned to the benefit of all in The Astral. Every Fragment, whether in The Lower or The Upper Levels of The Astral, is directly aware of what is occurring. Our thoughts and energies move exceedingly rapidly beyond physical measurement. For us it is natural, but for you, such energy would drive you insane. The human body, or any other species on Earth, is oscillating at a very low frequency, unlike our very high frequency that is not physical at all.

In the Sixth Plane of Evolution, most Collective Soul Groups are directly concerned with the expressions of the one you call The Creator, Our Prime Fragment. A Creator must be awakened to all aspects of life in any dimension and in any form. The amount of information that is processed, is beyond explanation here, since you are not able to imagine much.

Let us give you an example of fast sound. By playing *all* your favorite music at a speed, one hundred thousand times faster, in your time, would be for us, only one-second. All you would hear is a squeak. We hear all the songs you play as well all other music playing all over your planet at the same time, never misunderstanding a single word. So, when you pray, know we hear you and will come to your aide, in ways you cannot fathom, which may often leave you wondering what happened? Yet, deeply sensing you are changed in heart, mind, and body. Our ways of healing are always done with a transformation of our energy that stimulates change.

Now that you have a glimpse of the vibration we generate, you can begin to understand that when you ask us to materialize in front of you as a solid person, that this is indeed possible, provided your mind is oscillating at the same speed as us. In order for this to occur, we must slow ourselves down while you speed yourself up. In the world of energy, slower speed in physicality is faster, while in spiritual form, fast speed become slower when used to connect with those living on Earth.

A moment of such unity will happen when a Medium can surrender their body to us to use to speak. Otherwise, we will not connect. On occasions we will manifest as humans, speak a message, and leave, while the person receiving the message is left with a reminder of The Oneness, and their own transformed spiritual vibrational feeling, which soon dissipates after the visit is concluded. Usually the one we share with has a dream-like flash memory, that will never be forgotten, but which may take many years to pass, before what was shared is understood. In other words, the work that a person came to do eventually begins to make sense to them because of their encounter with an Ascended Master.

In order to manifest ourselves in human form in your times, we must focus on a life we have lived before, and manifest that appearance relative to the times, so our dress may be old fashioned for example. To become visible involves pulling on the dark density of form for us. Our spiritual energy becomes a mixture of Dark and Light Matter for you to see us clearly! Only those who are Ascended Masters appear when it is necessary. We often arrive with many on such an occasion, since a physical encounter is not the normal approach, and there are always students of The Light wanting to observe. A Medium will instantly know that their living room is crowded or that the hall they are giving a talk in, is filled with Light Spirits, who are busy working with the physical Humans while they open up to the wisdom that is channeled. Our point here, is to reveal that no one Fragment of the Oneness works alone. We are always united and active. The darker or denser the force, the lighter the glow of The Oneness.

As we said earlier, the Light of The Oneness is filled with friction that oscillates at such a high frequency, that it is infinite and constantly moving, darting around amid the dense dark energy, creating constant friction to maintain the continuance of The Oneness at all times. Imagine twenty spot lights being beamed up at the dark night sky when no moon shines. What you would see are patterns of light reflecting of one another and in various ways. Small explosions would be observed creating an appearance of a brighter light as they overlap. Without the Dark Matter, there would be no light seen. Without The Light, one would miss the existence of The Dark. It is always important to remember that The Light and The Dark are part of the same energy, which resonates and reverberates at different speeds, with different tones called musical notes. Your Universe if very musical. Sound is the key to your next energy source that will sustain life in a different way. As you all become more spiritual on Earth, so your vibrations will change, and the energy of your planet will become more vibrant.

Earth has its own resonations. Humans tap into it with electrical equipment that also resonates sound. Two combined sounds equals a measurement. This basic rule is in all life. As your technical knowledge improves, so you will all become aware how sound can be used to heal, create energy for warmth and cooling and so much more. There is still much of your world that you do not understand and have no clue as to how to use the natural flora and fauna to generate more energy, more food and more of anything else you wish to create.

Everywhere you look on Earth, you see patterns. Patterns are the key within The Divine Force, where energy can be heard as sound resonates and echo responses are captured. Around your planet are rings of energy. Some are formed from negative energy created by Human thoughts and from animal's natural instincts. Other sounds are trapped energy from times gone by, such as nuclear wars and bomb explosions. In opposite polarity, are the sounds of the ocean, the music you play and the voices that speak in harmony. We note here that those who are deaf, have an advantage over those who hear. They are trained to feel the vibrations of sound and to know and interpret it, and use it, to express self in ways not understood anatomically. What you call Psychometry, is for us, the normal way of living and working within The Oneness.

Those living on Earth embrace the Dark Side of nature, to establish a reality that is often adhered to for thousands of years. Meanwhile, we in the Oneness, absorb and dissolve energy consistently, moving on with the Creation of all that was, is, and will eventually become form in new physical and spiritual ways on Earth. We create an aspect of existence out there, as you would put it, for you to explore on Earth.

There is no hocus pocus to be done. There are no special magic potions to take. There is no race against time. Life is for living in the now, but few learn how to be patient and calm and to gently travel through life. Many are steeped in traditions that are ancient. How can one move on from the past when it is never allowed to dissolve back into the Oneness? Once again, we remind you that you are now fully embodied with the emanation of The Great Aquarian Age. This is the end of what was and the beginning of what will be. Put down your guns, your fists and open up to exploration. Love abounds when you learn to share and receive.

Spend time in contemplation in a garden. Look at the formation of all life forms around you. See the patterns of petals, leaves and the colors of life. Every pattern resonates a vibration. Every color is the physical form of a vibration. The more the vibration resonates, the lighter the color becomes. Consequently, when something is only densely resonating, the color is darker as indeed its musical notes are lower!

Your world places a great deal of emphasis on science and the study of vibrations. Whether you listen for sounds in space, or the rumblings of the magma in Earth's core, you are becoming acquainted with the need to know your own planet and its vibration. We will say here that there are planets where unity and vibration are in harmony. Perhaps one day you will incarnate there too.

So our summation of what light is, leaves us to reveal to you that it is the core of all that is the 'I Am' of existence, having first been generated by The Dark Side, when pressure and friction became so great, that it gave birth to light. Then there was a Universal awakening in knowing that as long as there is dark, there must also be light to exist in. This basic premise is felt, understood, and worked with on all Planes of Evolution.

In The Seventh Plane of Evolution, all Fragments are without identity, free of encumbrance of any planetary forms and ways and means. Here in this *infinite inner circle* creation is spontaneous, born out of need to be known and felt. Here energy is generated outward to all Fragments on all levels of existence. In these unique moments, The Oneness is truly united in one singular thought and feeling. I exist, I am, and all this is 'I, The One.' I am Love Divine, embraced by My Divine Love of experiences of all that I AM!

We stated earlier that circles of Light and Dark surround the

Earth. Since a human body is made biochemically from the materials of your planet we wish to end this chapter with the parallels that you all often forget about.

Each of you has a body that generates energy as you walk, talk, sing, dance or sit still and think. You are a living Aura of energy that extends from your physical body. Around your body is a force field of regenerating sound, that is the color of the states of your organs and body in general. If you are ill, it will be dark. Lying outside the physical body's energy is another swirling energy force field of thoughts and emotions you generate constantly about your life. This is called The Etheric Body, which is often unstable, resulting in an imbalance in personality and characteristics. When these two aspects of the Aura are in friction, you will feel hot and anxious. Along the outside of the Etheric Body, is the energy of your Spirit Body that is able to rebalance the first two Bodies. However, the Spirit Body can be weak, since the lower two aspects of the embodied-self are in conflict, causing separation in the auric field.

The Lower-self mentality and emotions are often in dispute about issues involving truth and justice. The Spirit Body's energy carries the DNA of Ancestors, your Soul Structure Coding and your fate or karma in this life, to follow a pathway you have previously decided upon before incarnation. This part of the Aura is often in need of repair and healing from The Oneness. A further layer of the outer Aura is The Higher Mind Body that generates awareness of actions happening in the existence of The Oneness. This resonating energy is then downloaded in easy forms or images, that will guide each individual along their chosen pathway. The final aspect of the Aura is the outer edge where the Soul Body's energy is entwined with its Soul Group. This Soul Body provides an ebb and flow of spiritual healing energy to ensure life continues on Earth. This form of energized light in physical contact provides assistance from The Oneness.

In this way, each incarnated Fragment is to be constantly assisted in awareness of the journey each takes. When harmonizing and rebalancing the entire Aura, emotional and mental states are neutrally entwined allowing a replenishment in the physical body. When you rejuvenate and regrow cells, it is your DNA coding that will heal your body. The ultimate lesson here is, to be as interactive and as aware as possible of both the dark and the light sides of self, and how to use both to bring about a change in the way this world continues in the future. Yes, we are all different, yet united by The One Prime Fragment as one unit. We all want life in all its forms to continue.

To embrace this world, is to accept the colors, the good and bad happenings, along with the transformations of all species as they happen. Currently you are finally learning to integrate your species. In time, a wholeness of life and living will emerge, but until then, take notice how you vocally sound when happy or sad. Remember you are generating sound, even if you do not say a word aloud!

From a different point of view, we too are constantly in transition as our aura's change. The primary coding is always active in every Fragment, no matter whether they are in the Dark Side or The Light Side. Friction is the living force that we all need to create in order to survive, and to evolve within The Oneness and its continuation.

To finalize all Fragments are a collection of light sparks that shimmer and shine, often stimulated by dark patches of energy that are transforming in what you might call anatomic fusion. To see us in light mode is fleeting, but often never forgotten.

We referred to the rings of energy around you Planet. Liken to your Aura, your Earth has the same layers of Ascension built into its land, oceans and all creatures that live there. All these collective energies of survival, whether of Earth, Humans, Animals, Insects, or old archaic forms who lived in fear, pain, anger, loss, and guilt or in appreciation of the existence of life, are memories entrapped in your upper hemispheres. As you leave Earth's atmosphere, you pass into The Oneness and The Astral Levels of Evolution that are mirror-images to us all. In this way, we learn a great deal more about our existence.

CHAPTER FIVE
The Rainbow Effect

It is said that one cannot stand at the end of a rainbow, but that is not the case, since Dr. Margaret was able to have this experience when she was in her tenth year, while playing with her friends. When she stood in the rainbow with her friends, they could see tiny specks of multicolor droplets on their arms and clothing. She also experienced static electrical discharges of energy that prickled and comfortably discharged negative energy from her body. This unique experience was truly an amazing event for them all.

By understanding the above, you will begin to contemplate an awareness of just how much static energy you produce yourself. Static energy, known as electrical discharges, are caused by heat versus cold when dark versus light come together in friction, generating a formed arc with static energy arising on the surface of the Earth. In like manner, when you are emotionally and mentally at odds with yourself, you are generating a static energy in your aura that can affect others, who will tingle uncomfortably as you shout and mope about an issue. Yes, you are whipping up a storm in your aura!

When you hold two opposing magnets near one another, there is a repelling action. When you unite North and South Poles of two magnets, there is an interaction and a reaction that is usually very positive. The energy of both create circles in patterns that can be proven with iron filings. Now, let us take this lesson a little bit further in order to explain to you how we, in The Oneness, interact with one another. In some senses, it is no different from a psychic working with a client. They use their Spirit essence to feel, sense, know and help a person. In the Spirit World, as you call it, we are actively creating energy that produces static discharges that can be used to further the existence of The Oneness.

When you realize that everything created is geometrical, and in that form, generates vibrations that consistently flow outward, it must be also understood that energy must be drawn into the form too. Static electrical discharges provide an exchange of energy needed. Too much negativity will repel the light, while too much light will dissipate and eventually disappear, just like the rainbow. So what is it that keeps our Spirits consistently alive and ebbing with new energy to share? We are in a sense, each likened to a rainbow. Our forms constantly change, causing us to shift awareness as input arrives from our Soul Groups. We know what they are all about, without having to question anything. This all-knowing aspect of self is liken to a computer in your world. Much of who we are remains hidden, while we show the parts of us that you need to see.

If you actually sit in front of a computer to search for information, you are easily exposed to millions of choices, which mostly likely will not be seen by you, since you will pay attention to the first ten items. Then make a choice and work with that choice. Here in The Oneness, we are exposed to the millions of inputs, all of which we listen to, observe, and interact with, when necessary. The result of our ways of interacting vary according to the needs of our students. Students can be in the Oneness, or on Earth in respect to the nature of this book. It should be also realized that we have connections with many other Universes and they, in turn, have their own way of connecting with The Dark & The Light in the functionality of their species.

When we open up in The Oneness to the streams of messages that are sent to us, we receive them in both dark and light ways. Instantly, we respond and apply the best modalities to assist, no matter the problem.

Here are a few examples.

#1: A child lies in a cold clammy sweat, while fighting off the Measles disease. What the doctor sees is a gravely ill child, who is likely to develop Meningitis and possibly death. What we see is that the child's Five aspects of the Aura are in conflict as static energy heats up the body. As soon as we rebalance the Spirit Body, the lower and higher aspects of the Aura become balanced and the fever subsides. When a child is very young, their emotions lead the way. If sorrow and misery are a daily experience, then the Etheric Body will be so overloaded with dark energy, when the Spirit Body cannot recover a balance. Hence our interference in the healing process. We can shift energy in any situation, provided the person to be healed is wanting it.

#2: A man sits in his chair reading a spiritual book. He is eager to absorb all that is written, but he tires as he reads, and soon he is drifting into sleep. His mind is dreaming about what he has read, while his body relaxes into the chair. In that moment, he is receptive to us and ready for a dream. In that dream, we give him deeper answers to his questions. As he dreams, he sees the colors of the light and the magic of healing. His aura has shifted and when he awakens, he feels refreshed and more insightful about the book he has read so far. In this simple dream with us he has learned to love himself and all that he does. Much later, he will write his own book with our help. Yes, Channeling is a state of unity where color abounds with many minds in unity.

It should be noted here that some deaths are part of the *Universal Pattern of Change*. These universal patterns of change occur every year in your world. They can be very simple, almost unnoticed, to very obvious, such as the return of the Corona Virus, now released from the once frozen waters of the North & South Poles. This newly awakened virus can mutate and survive well in any climate, since it generates its own life force every second. In the example of the above rainbow effect, this virus is constantly transforming and shifting its purpose and function, generating a different vibration. Originally it was designed to protect the planet from bacteria that was destructive to the races who lived on Earth. Now, eons of ages later, it has been released to a race of people with none of the original forms that lived long ago. Your bio-genetic coding is different from those who went before you. However, your bio-genetic reproductive abilities in all five systems of your body, do have the remnants of those ages gone by. Those with ancient DNA are more likely to survive, than newer races made later.

All Old Souls who incarnate are generally following a line of ancestry in their DNA from not just hundreds of years, but of thousands! Each person carries the marks of prior lives as well as a strong connection with the Oneness. These people are leaders of your world, who will make their mark in your history. No matter their cause, journey, or successes and failures, you will only remember bits and pieces that conveniently help you at that moment in time. Much later, little is recalled unless it is set in writing. When someone is directed to awaken a memory, then that news is shared, and with it comes a new understanding, that in turn, changes everyone's opinion. Illnesses and diseases have a way of marking time, but few truly understand the glory of a single moment when a new idea turns into a form that can be used by everyone.

All over your planet, people are using the internet. Someone in a small room is busy making up a new program relative to their own need. As time passes, more and more people learn to use that new program and the original developer is long forgotten, but his work goes on until someone else comes up with a better program, and then the old one is cast aside. In every case of evolvement, there is always a rainbow effect on the many who adapt and move on. Looking down on the heads of all, we see many rainbows of colors in your auras. You must remember that as long as you are moving and your brain and body is working, you are releasing colors that cause others to vibrate either in discord or harmony. The psychic sense of Psychometry is a constant in all aspects of life resources. Even a flower can feel you coming when you walk along a pathway. The sentient energy of life is always discharged in a rainbow effect, whether in dark or light colors. The pattern of colors is far greater in our world of The Oneness, since we have many more musical keys and notes to play with, that are beyond your normal hearing, feeling, or knowing.

If an Ascended Master wishes to enter the Second Plane on the sixth level to help a Fragment to ascend to the next level, that Master must take on the lower vibrations of sound and color in order to be seen by the Fragment they have come to save. In the same way, we Archangels must adapt our energy into a lower vibration and color for you to see us. The danger of entering the Dark, is to lose the light in self. This is why we prepare thoroughly in the moment to do the right thing for every Fragment on any *Level of Evolution*. Our unique ways of helping have been adapted over eons of time as the species living on Earth have come and gone. It is important at this juncture in this book to know that what was, is no longer appropriate to the evolving life on your planet.

Now that we have fully described the rainbow effect, we wish you to apply this to your way of life. When you pick up a heavy parcel, you know you use your muscles, but now it is time to think about how much energy you are using and wasting in discharges that create minute rainbows in your aura, as energy moves away from your body passing through the Etheric, Spirit, Higher Mind and Soul Bodies of the Aura. As energy leaves the Aura, an explosive discharge can be captured outside your Aura by a paranormal photographer. Dr. Margaret has many such photos taken my Stephen Van Coops many years ago.

Bearing in mind how the rainbow effect is active on every Plane of Evolution, it should be understood that patterns of existence, create patterns of light, which in turn created miniscule to giant rainbows across the Universes of the Cosmos. There are places in the Cosmos where it appears no light shines to your eyes, but to other species, their light is of a different vibration and easily seen. As you know, a cat can see in the dark, so other species in existence can see light in the dark on their planet.

As Ascended Ones, we are able to shift our energy to suit the circumstances of the planets we visit, the Fragments we help, as well as to create new species as the Prime Fragment determines collectively throughout all that exist in any dimension.

Since you can now begin to understand the vastness of space, you may well begin to acknowledge just how magnificent all is, that has thus far been created. Yet there have always been Fragments who have somehow been lost. You could call them Fallen Angels from times when Souls incarnated to explore without purpose, and still others with purpose who became bonded and tied to Earth. Those Fallen Angels are called Succubus, who laid with women or men to induce physical forms. At that time it was considered a good way to teach Earthlings to become aware of their Soul. Fortunately, this plan worked, but at the expense of losing some of our upper angelic Fragments who were unprepared for what was to come! The first destruction of the surface of Earth caused them to develop earthly ways to survive when nothing much was left. Yes, A new beginning of a new race of Species was begun, and with it our search to find our brothers and sisters of Soul.

In those days, a new plan surfaced to always find every Fragment that was missing and still it goes on as explained in an earlier chapter. The result of this was the development of the Soul Groups. When many Souls bond together in a common cause, there is a powerful energy exchange amid all Universes. Planets are transformed, worlds are restructured, and life is challenged. Most of our plans for your time on your planet are thousands of years old, but very appropriate for The Great Aquarian Age. There is an army of lightworkers now incarnated. Each is encoded with The Oneness's plans and will, in their own way and time, manifest the next step of evolution on your planet which will benefit those still living.

As your world shifts, embracing The Great Aquarian Age, the circles of darkness around your planet will shift and with it the phases of the moon will alter color as you see it. In like manner, your energies in the Aura of every human will also change. An awakening of skills and abilities will manifest new cultures, ways and means of doing business and of celebrating life. A new vibration will exist, causing all life to embrace a new style of living. Anything that Mankind can imagine will be possible once the mind and heart agree and creativity then abounds.

Light workers, as you call them, exist in all Planes of Evolution. By choice, they keep the balance active within the center of all that is. The Core of The Oneness is where all aspects of all existences are united in one aspect of Divine Existence. 'I AM!' There, a light show is constant and with it, arises many new awakenings that are conceived and later manifested in a variety of ways.

CHAPTER SIX
The Soul Structure Coding

Though we have explained the structure of the Soul Coding in many other books written by Dr. Margaret, we must now explain it from a different point of view. In all her books, we have explained how this coding is developed in personality along with direction and purpose in each life lived. We have explained how your emotional and mental attitude is formed, through an awakening in the womb to the DNA of your coding in ancestors and from The Oneness in spiritual coding for a journey in life to be completed. You may like to read: *The Rejection Syndrome* for a fuller understanding of your earthly ways and conditioning.

Here in this chapter, we must explain how it is programmed into every Fragment that is fully awakened to their Divine Presence in The Oneness. But first, we must remind you that the Laws Of Karma apply throughout the entire structure and all forms of The Oneness. While these rules appear to not be broken, it is paramount that they are constantly used and tested to their limits in order for friction to manifest and for spiritual growth to occur. These Five Laws Of Karma have existed since the dawn of time on your planet and elsewhere not known to you.

Laws Of Karma:

1. No Fragment may impose its will on another at any time, on any Level

2. Each Fragment shall be responsible for all it creates in positive and negative actions

3. Each Fragment shall share itself with all other Fragments in unconditional love

4. Each Fragment shall attract like in the mirror image, either in opposition or support for growth without judgment

5. Each Fragment shall in unconditional love, surrender to The Creator.

In The Oneness, whether in the First Plane of darkness and creation, or the Seventh Plane of Ascension and further creations, there are in your understanding, forty-nine Levels to ascend through. On every Level, there must be some form of co-operation and interaction with these laws to create friction, resonation, and reverberation, allowing a transformation of energy in every Fragment throughout all that is collectively active or passive in The Oneness.

From an earthly point of view, let us explain some aspects of the Soul Structure coding and how it applies and affects every Fragmented Soul in Evolution. We will begin with *The Chief Features* and descend from the Seventh Plane down to the First Plane.

The Chief Features are all dynamic in form. Their purpose is to cause controversy and disorder, while teaching lessons of alternative ways and means to find inner peace, and spiritual senses of belonging to The Oneness. The *Seven Chief Features* are primal and have successfully assisted Fragments to evolve throughout all forty-nine levels.

The Chief Features are: *Greed, Arrogance, Self-Destruction, Self-Deprecation, Impatience, Martyrdom and Stubbornness.* Each has a negative and positive side to it, which has in Ages past, caused a fearful disruption within The Oneness, resulting in a need for control and balance.

When *Greed* first arose, it stimulated Fragments in a variety of ways to understand the entirety of *egotism* verses *voracity*. In the Seventh Plane of Evolution, the 'I AM' self of the Prime Fragment was upset by the many influences of all Fragments in the Lower Planes including Earth. There was a constant need to rebalance the expressions of wanting more, getting more and also of letting things pass away into oblivion. When Fragments in the lower Planes of Evolution were inactive, then discourse caused disassociations, which then easily undermined the awareness of all that is. So The Laws of Karma were created to keep the balance. If such an occasion arises again, The Oneness would prevent the collapse of command as it were!. On this seventh level, many Fragments exist to simply aide the Prime Fragment to remain in balance. Following the primal laws of karma manifested on Earth, all Fragments on this Seventh Plane of Evolution are always constantly reflecting and adapting to keep all aspects of creation in harmony between the Lower and Upper Planes of Evolution to ensure the balance of the whole.

Long ago, *Greed* was discovered when Fragments broke away from The Oneness to seek their own destiny. Those lost to the Oneness, are still being recovered and helped to return and reunite in sharing more input to the consciousness of The Oneness's existence. There is no blame or shame. Only a longing to be whole, entices and unites the Fragment to become one with all that is. Their return reminds all that *voracious* energy creates separation and a lack of friction. The *First Law of Karma* was introduced to prevent separation. This allows each Fragment to be in its own space to explore, and when done, to return to the fold when it wishes. No other Fragment can make them return, since it is known that each Fragment knows, through *egotism*, when it needs to return to be a part of The Oneness in all that is occurring.

As Fragments incarnated in various forms, not yet defined in those periods of The Oneness's existence, *Arrogance* manifested in the forms of *pride* versus *vanity*. If you could use your imagination to become a king of a Castle, how would you want things to be? You would have many ideas, along with emotional desires to manifest lots of things in the style of your choosing. This very dominant trait was a great test for the Prime Fragment, being filled with new discoveries that each Fragment played with. As a result of this awakening, the *Second Law of karma* was created for all Fragments to follow. Each Fragment was made responsible for all that it did, good or bad, and was joyfully accepted as one who tested the strength of The Oneness and all it stands for.

The Chief Feature of Arrogance brought *pride* consciousness in all that one achieved. *Pride* was not seen as bad, but as a stimulant to discover more about self and each's capability in mastery of things created. For some *vanity* in competition arose, causing the Prime Fragment to awaken to self-importance as commander and leader. As a result of discord over ways and means of manifesting too much or too little, a new law was added. The *Third Law of Karma* was introduced establishing rules to share and love unconditionally, all aspects of spiritual and physical growth, in any situation. This allowed the Prime Fragment to delegate and observe. Thus acquiring some freedom of inner peace and sanctuary.

Meanwhile, a new awareness evolved into the *Chief Feature of Self-Destruction*, which came unexpectedly when Fragments in the lower Plane of Darkness were feeling forgotten. Though this was not a reality, it was considered a very negative place to visit for those Fragments who were residing within the Seventh Plane of Evolution. This caused many Fragments within the Second Plane to rebel. Imagine a revolution that becomes destructive at its source, founded on false information. Such was the way of this level in The Oneness, when many Fragments sacrificed their forms in rebellion, becoming fixed in those forms for all time. Then the opposite occurred since all forms were now fixed, nothing was happening, and the Second Plane of Evolution was slowly disintegrating.

Since the Prime Fragment loved all Fragments who are a part of itself, a new understanding was released; that of love and expansion of inner joy. As a result, many Fragments experienced death and rejuvenation of life to awaken once again within the arms of The Oneness. Their Souls were reborn. Here the first healing was revealed to all Fragments within The Oneness, which today still exists for all. This *Third Law of Karma* was considered a true awakening of The Oneness, and the beginning of a new era in consciousness to manifest more insightful events. All Fragments embraced sharing self with other Fragments in unconditional love.

What followed was a general awakening to a state of alarm, as the *Chief Feature of Self-deprecation* manifested, pushing all Fragments who had begun to understand 'The Way of The Oneness,' to perceive its own journey, that it must take, to find a sense of self in *humility.* Since no Fragment had been taught to be humble, often arguments and disorder arose in the Third and Fourth Planes of Evolution, where conflict was constant, causing a great deal of friction to be harmonized and used. Here personalities developed along with states of *abasement,* where *Greed, Arrogance* and *Self-destruction* were combined to cause new lessons in *Self-destruction* which in turn led to *Self-deprecation.* What was good, seemed to be bad and vice versa. A new wave of terror hit the Oneness and once again, the Prime Fragment had to reassess and rebalance the entirety of all energy that was amassing as eons of time passed, unmeasurable to The Oneness.

It was then that the *Fourth Law of Karma* was introduced. Every Fragment was now called a Soul and every Soul was expected to incarnate in form on Planet Earth or elsewhere in order to invent, create and destroy all manner of forms. You could say that The Oneness was finally ready to evolve in a time when creation could no longer just focus on what was within it, but now needed to focus on what was outside of the normal.

With many Fragmented Souls wanting to incarnate and explore other forms, it was necessary to create this *Fourth Law of karma* to ensure that every Fragment will, no matter the circumstance, remember to love and honor one another, and if necessary, to accept their differences, knowing that they are all part of The Oneness in experimentation of learning new ways to exist. This law ensured that all Fragments were equal to one another and connected at all times, no matter the circumstance. Today you see this happening in your world when a famous person dies suddenly. Everyone mourns the loss and identifies with that person, each conceiving themselves as supporters, finding ways to carry on in the vane of the seeds that were laid during this person's lifetime.

This *Fourth Law Of Karma* also supports the *Chief Feature of Impatience* for those who incarnate. Life on Planet Earth is not easy for anyone. You all have the *audacity* to believe you are in charge of your lives, but rarely are you all happy together. Constantly there are challengers, and many become *intolerant* of others as you judge and condemn them. So, this law was established to ensure that judgment will always be over-ruled with love for one another. However, it was made abundantly clear that many Souls who incarnated, were too generous and giving was often abused. Those who appeared to demonstrate *selflessness* were often judged and condemned for being too perfect, while others were suffering in fear of *mortification* which often did include death and destruction. The Oneness discovered

The *Chief Feature of Martyrdom!* Despite the existence of this Fourth Law of Karma, many wars were fought on Earth or in the skies. Too many Fragments died and the recovery in The Oneness was painful and long. Yet there was better times to come.

In the witnessing of such tyranny on Earth, The Prime Fragment provided the last *Law of Karma,* which was to love God, The Prime Fragment, in unconditional love and support for The Oneness to continue, in all Its glory. Even as you live today, in a variety of ways and means, when individuals appear to be considered arrogant, greedy, impatient, and stubborn, they cause unrest! There are still those who through Self-destruction, Self-deprecation and Martyrdom remind you to find the balance between the dark and light of self.

The last Chief Feature of *Stubbornness* was attached to The Fifth Law of Karma, in that The Prime Fragment had *determination* and yes, even *obstinacy* to establish leadership with flexibility, in mirror-image of The Prime Fragment. This final aspect of leadership manifested so that law and order was finally established for all Fragments on any Level of Evolution.

We wish you to realize now that the combination of the *Laws of Karma* and the Coding of the *Chief Feature* within your *Soul Structure Coding* is working every second you are awake or asleep.

The Soul Structure Coding is explained in a book we channeled with Dr. Margaret called *Discover Your Baby's Spirit.* We mention it here since we are not concerned with sharing with you any information at this time with your lower self or earthly self. We are only here to share the evolution of Descension and Ascension that prioritizes The Oneness's continuation.

Each Fragment incarnates with a Soul Structure Coding that defines who they will become, along with their personal focus on life, and the priorities of The Oneness. When a Fragment prepares to be born in a certain century on Earth, they will chose to use their own Archetype, encoded when first created in the First Plane of Evolution, or choose to use a second Archetype as a mask. Ascended Masters may incarnate with several masks, using many aspects of the Archetypes known as Sage, Artisan, Priest, Slave, King, Warrior or Scholar. A Sage for example could wear the mask of a Slave and appear weak, but within the spiritual consciousness, they will be testing other Fragments who are incarnated and living with them.

Every Fragment must also choose a *Goal*, which can be the Primal Fragments choice. For example, The Oneness may be focusing on recovery of love and directly require many Fragments in a *Soul Group* to incarnate and express the *Goal of Rejection*, thus teaching a lesson of *discrimination*, versus *prejudice*. While still other Fragments group together with *Acceptance* as their *Goal* to learn to live in agape (joy) or negatively to express in *ingratiation.* The remaining *Goals*, that a fragment can chose from are, *Growth, Retardation, Dominance, Submission* or *Stagnation.* Any one of these chosen *Goals* will interface with every other Fragment on any Level of every Plane of Evolution. No one is ever alone when they incarnate.

Fragments working in the Upper Levels of The Fifth and Sixth Planes of Evolution are busy, in various ways, creating new toys for Humans and animals to work with. You can say that all these Ascended Fragments, called various names, such as The Holy Host, The Brotherhood, Ascended Master and Angels and Archangels, spend time developing new ways to help every Fragment to understand the power and value of being entwined within The Oneness. We Archangels are messengers who bring you learning and news. We have never requested faith, hope or trust in us, yet you do, and we appreciate your bonding with us within these pages. To answer your silent questions, we all have mastered our individual aspects of using the entire Soul Structure Codings of not only our own lives lived, but of all other fragments too. You can now begin to understand how much experience we all have in amalgamating all experiences of all Fragments as our own experiences too. We are the reflection of all that you have experienced and more.

Here on the Sixth Plane of Evolution, we all function in harmony. Divine Love and Wisdom flows from us to your spiritual Crown and Heart Centers, where you have also been encoded within your Soul Structure Coding. Everything you require for this life is prepared for you. Not everything you ask for is good for you. When we do not respond, know that we are protecting you from your selfish needs and the needs of others who would abuse you. When you are in harmony with your life's journey, you will receive all that you need. As we trust you, so we ask you to trust us.

Every Fragment was originally encoded with a Prime Archetype. Each Archetype was a copy of The Ascended Maters. In your world, for all human species, you are nurtured by the Seven Archangels, as earlier shared in this book. We seven Archangels have sub-divided as was the original coding in our birthing, allowing us to bring our consciousness into form. Our Archetype gave you personality and character in the form of sound vibration which allows you to know us by vibration and reverberation. Our present to you is our gift of Divine Nature that never changes. If you were created a Sage, then you will always be encoded as a Sage through all incarnations. However, you can borrow any of the other personalities from the other six Archetypes, thus giving you exploration and passion to learn. You have all evolved diligently, and we are grateful for your existence. Remember, your life is vital to the continued existence of The Oneness.

CHAPTER SEVEN
The Fifth Plane of Evolution

This Plane of Evolution is a very complicated one. All that is experienced on Earth is shared among the Fragments who have never incarnated, or who have lived on Earth for short periods of time to bring insightful knowledge of the Divine Purpose. You could call them Gurus, Priest, Teachers or Healers. Their philosophy and expression in life always leaves a marked impression on their pupils who continue their work, after they leave. All aspects of all forms of life are explored, categorized, and assessed with regard to the influence a life has had, not only on Earth, but throughout The Oneness. To ensure that each incarnated Fragment is able to remember, feel, and interact with The Oneness, the Soul Structure Coding of the individual Spirit, is vital to the continuation of feedback to the Fifth Plane of Evolution. Many of the Ascended Masters are directly connected with their interns on Earth. They will continually guide the Fragment to accomplish their Goal, and to overcome their issues as they arise.

In most cases, a Fragment will find a change occurring in their mid-life incarnation, when their Spirit is stimulated by their encoded Spirit Soul Coding. It is important here, to understand that an awakening of the spiritual consciousness leads to a change in personality traits. When a person is very negative in the first half of life, with the effective help of Spirit Guides, they will emerge into the Light and awaken to new understandings about life on Earth, from a new point of view. You may recall that some prisoners have been shut away for life, but during their time there, have awakened and written some very informative books. Yes, often life requires a period of silence within the conscious mind, which then allows the inner Spirit's consciousness to awaken. More information can be read in *The Rejection Syndrome* concerning this programming in a Human.

In this chapter, we will focus on how the Archetypal coding from us, and the coding from the Master Teachers in the Fifth Plane were collaged in Oneness. Before a Fragment incarnates, preparation begins. Many Fragments, sometime a Soul Group, will congregate and discuss a plan that is always concerned with the journey of Ascension for all Fragments. With each Fragment having a Primal single coding from its beginning, it will ensure that the focus of assimilation is absolute and equally shared among all Fragments. There are no secrets or misgivings in The Oneness. These plans are made in The Astral.

If a Human incarnates and becomes a killer, they will suffer in death and return to The Fifth Level of The Upper Astral, where they are assisted with investigating and expressing the nature of their Dark Side Self. In knowing that what they did, has left a lasting memory for years to come after they have left Earth, there is a sense of loss! These killers could be very old Souls, testing themselves in the dark side of human nature, while also testing many other Fragments who encountered this Human. Likewise a sweet natured person, being kind and loving, tragically dies, leaving another message in the values of life and things done. Old Souls may incarnate again and again, to continue the foray happening on Earth, at a later times, perhaps centuries later on Earth.

In order to have a personality befitting a Fragment's cause on Earth, they choose aspects of The Soul Structure Coding that will develop a personality based on ancestors, now Spirit Fragments, Spirit Guides and friends who will bond and directly contact, and influence, the incarnated Spirit to follow their pathway, in a personality befitting the Universal Plan, for your period in history. Since billions of Fragments are being born and dying now in your time, you can begin to understand just how busy this Fifth Level in The Astral has become. You could say that one is constantly climbing up a ladder, only to have to climb down immediately, over and over again, and when ready, will ascend to The Fifth Plane of Evolution. The Forth Plane of Evolution is a reflection of both The Lower and Upper Astral levels, stimulated by the Upper three Levels in The Third Plane of Evolution and the lower four Levels of The Fifth Plane of Evolution. You can see here that these two Planes of Evolution are closely entwined to assure energy continue to move throughout The Oneness,

The Fifth Plane of Evolution never rests. All experiences are passed to the Lower Forth Astral Plane or on up to The Sixth Plane. The Fifth Plane is akin to a sorting house where what comes in, must go out. When one exists within the Seven Levels of this Plane of Evolution, there are continual experiences being completely and utterly explored, in all ways possible, from a spiritual point of view. In a sense, this Plane is the engine that drive the force ever on to keep The Oneness active and functioning productively. When reading this, imagine you are watching thousands of movies at once and all are remembered in great detail. If you could do this, you would remember every bodily expression, emotion, thought and, of course, hopes and dreams of all the characters in each movie. In some way, you would assimilate them all, and in time, find a new story, built out of the old ones. What you would see here, is the amalgamation of all stories into one big movie that can never be tossed aside, since it speaks of the hearts of all species on Earth.

For a Fragment to become aware of its existence on Earth, it is encoded with three aspects called *Modes*; There are seven *Modes* to choose from when incarnating: *Power, Caution, Passion, Repression, Aggression, Perseverance and Observation.* Each Mode has a dark and light side to it. Here is an example, A Mode of *Power* is expressed through the Heart Chakra, while the Mode of *Inspiration* is expounded through *Passion* in the Throat Chakra and with the final Mode Of *Action* for the body to display

Aggression. A person with this complex coding, would be a very active person in either a very negative or positive way, where deeds done would not go unnoticed. With the demonstration of *Power*, a Fragment would demonstrate either *Authority* or *Oppression.* While expressing *Passion* a Fragment can *intellectually self-actualize* their plan and *identify* their mistakes. When their plan is put into *action* they could show traits of *Dynamism or Belligerence.*

If we were to explain all the working of the other Modes in examples, we would be writing hundreds of books, showing millions of different personalities, since free will, is a big part of the evolution of the personality in any one Fragment. If a person has *Caution, Repression,* and *Perseverance* encoded, then that Fragment would, from a spiritual point of view, often sink into state of *Deliberation,* or likely, become *Phobic!* With constant attention paid to *Restraint* and *Inhibition,* this Fragment would be constantly stimulating self to continue searching with *Persistence*, to find a cure while staying fixed in pain and emotional anguish, thus displaying the inordinate *immutability* of a fixed state of mind.

The final *Mode* for spiritual assimilation is *The Mode* of *Observation* which provides an opportunity to live life, in such a way, as to perceive *Clarity* enhanced by *Surveillance* of all aspect of life. In this way, the incarnated Fragment can outgrow old habits and ideas, to effectively expand life's points of view. When these Seven Modes are considered and accepted in The Oneness, the incarnating Fragment will be changed accordingly. Choice is made to never repeat personal history acquired throughout all their previous lives lived. They must search for a new way to evolve on Earth. Even if two incarnating Fragments have the same Modes, with similar encoded DNA of ancestors and the spiritual bonding that was done in The Oneness before embodiment, there never is a copycat performance on Earth, as each engages in activities with different perceptions.

Since The Oneness is constantly changing as energy shifts, moved by friction and unity, this must be repeated on Earth. When a Spirit Fragment enters life in the womb after the quickening, there is a bonding, in the physical sense, between the Mother and Child on a spiritual level. Their individual Soul Structure Codings entwine within their combined Auras. This sharing provides the mother with peaceful healing, while the Spirit Fragment is absorbing the mother's journey thus far, with regard to both her negative and positive points of view. In this way, the child starts out life being exactly like the mother, until the birthing and bonding stage is over. By the time a child reaches the closure of his/her first year, autonomy has begun and with it, an awakening of the child's own encoded *Modes* that will develop into ways of *Expression, Inspiration, Action* and *Assimilation.* Both Mother and Child will be closely connected to their Archangel, Angels, Spirit Guides, and others.

While the above bonding is completing, *The Attitudes* that are encoded with both the Mother and Child will collage. *The Seven Attitudes* provide periods of lifestyles, beliefs, happenings, and ways in processing information about life in general. However, each has a *Primary Attitude* that has been shared in the womb *The Attitudes* are: *Idealist, Skeptic, Spiritualist, Stoic, Realist, Cynic and Pragmatist.* Yet again, each type of *Attitud*e has both negative and positive traits.

If two Fragments, now Spirits, have both incarnated with the same spiritual coding of one *Primal Attitude,* then life will likely turn out to be a rollercoaster of agreeing and disagreeing, since each perceives the world differently. If a Mother and child have different *Primal Attitudes,* then there is likely to be a great deal of adapting going on. As time passes, each Human will grow with different focuses in how they see life, since their physical attitudes are stimulated to manifest in the character of each. A child and mother can grow apart or become closer, relative to the input from other family members, friends and yes, enemies too, with the influences of RNA intake being assimilated as fact or fiction.

When a child grows up, their earthly emotional attitudes change with the times, but each child will adapt those early attitudes by assimilating all that has happened into an overview, relative to the periods of history outlined with their Soul Structure Coding. Each *Attitude* chosen is embedded within the Soul Structure Coding, providing cycles of years where perspectives on lifestyles change with experience. For example, one could move through years of being a *Realist,* expanding *perceptions* while often in *supposition.* The Book, *The Rejection Syndrome* explains this more fully, allowing human nature to explore and discover new aspects of self on a daily basis.

We will now over-turn this earthly consciousness of *The Attitudes.* In *The Fifth Plane of Evolution* there is no time! The encoded *Attitudes* take on a different role; that of psychology where the power of Ascension or Descension becomes the overall concern. Since there is no judgment in the Oneness, one must acknowledge concerns in how the energy of The Oneness is keeping in balance with all evolving Fragments, that are returning to the fold, along with those Fragments that are leaving to be born. In your world, one Fragment dies as another is born every second. The Forth Plane of Evolution is very busy too.

Because the Forth & Fifth Planes are constantly entwined, a great deal of energy is exchanged that can cause an amazing shift in experiences, where all Fragments in The Oneness are affected, and in agreement to change and transform all that was bad ,into all that is good, or vice versa. In such a case, Fragments throughout all forty-nine Levels of The Planes of Evolution will become involved with expressive regenerated energy, relative to their Plane, where they each refocus and balance their collective consciousness into a new form, thus creating friction while, emanating heat and light within. Often there can be an energy battle to control the pressure of the Light and Dark elements of change.

In this type of situation, when The Dark and The Light battle for supremacy, there is no winner! Only change manifests, and with change a unification dawns, as the Oneness allows energy to find its own balance. If any eruptions of energy do occur, *The Fifth Plane of Evolution* will be super active in maintaining a balance. When both negative and positive responses occur at the same time on Earth, a battle of pressures arises causing a rift not only on Earth, but throughout the Cosmos. During such times of conflict, when an eruption occurs within *The Universal Force,* the balance of energy is greatly disturbed. When Universal energy is disrupted, friction occurs, causing a new dynamic event to happen, somewhere in the Cosmos, and throughout the Oneness. The result of the eruption in The Oneness is an awakening of all Fragments into developing a new focus on form and function.

Since The Oneness has created all forms, Earth is affected too. You could say, you will likely experience storms, ocean flooding, earthquakes, meteorite showers and earthly battles etc. that happen suddenly or creep up slowly over your time, until for example, a great war begins where the battle of the Oneness is physically fought. During such a time, the Oneness is absorbing and reforming what will become your future planet reborn. Such a grand revolution is like a breath of fresh air. Acceptance of change is always welcome in The Oneness. As you say, move on and let go of the past, we say, let go of all that was and start afresh reforming old energy into new forms.

Currently, we are all approaching this magnificent time of change when all that you hold dear will disappear, leaving room for new creations, styles of living, and an awakening of a new type of philosophy, that will stir the souls of all fragments to unite in love and joy. A new understanding of being in existence will flow into the hearts of all as it is realized that the continuation of Ascension and Descension is assured. Those on the Forth Plane of Evolution will live, die, and reincarnate with new Soul Structure Codings, that stimulate imagination and acceptance of change, while focused on unity of their existence and in acceptance of the changes to come.

Since this chapter if more about The Fifth Plane of Evolution, we would like to clarify the *Attitudes,* from the point of view of an Ascended Master. Because every Human is connected with many Spirit Fragments both on Earth and in The Astral, there are many other Fragments that are entwined within their ancestor's history still. They work diligently to help the newly incarnated descendants survive. These spiritual interactions form a very important part of energy exchanges between Earth and The Astral, that is constantly like a bouncing ball, showing no control of direction or flow. It then becomes obvious that something must be done to prevent an imbalance, and so the Fifth Plane of Evolution will control that bouncing ball by giving it purpose.

Ascended Masters and the Upper Echelon of the Prime Fragment's supporters do stimulate changes in energy, by creating sound waves that generate a vibrational change in consciousness as well as in form. These Ancient Ones, knowing what has gone before, are able to manipulate forms into new vibrational shapes that will manifest new forms in times to come.

Though the old ways are long gone from Earth, many Ascended Fragments are still locked into the history of the lessons of the Piscean Age. It is, therefore, necessary for The Ancient

Ones to release their control within the Fifth Plane, allowing energy to settle and to reveal a better solution for all concerned. What follows is a desire to rebuild, restructure and reprogram the united lessons that are encoded into all Fragments of The Oneness. You might call it a New Age Of Enlightenment. We shall simply say, 'The New Dawn of The Great Aquarian Age' is upon you. So expect to connect with new Spirit Guides and have new friends on Earth. Become aware that you have choices not known before and should be in acceptance of alternative ascended ways that The Oneness will reveal within itself to you.

CHAPTER EIGHT
Our Roles & Connections As Ascended Masters, The Higher Arche & Soul Groups

As was stated earlier in this book, we Archangels were developed as the catalyst between all sources of energy in The Oneness and the creation of Form not only on Earth, but also elsewhere, not conceded by Humans until now. In this chapter we will share more about our interactions between The Seventh Plane of Evolution and your Fourth Plane of Evolution.

In The Higher Arche of the Seventh Plane of Evolution, from your point of view, we wish to turn our previous concept upside down and ask you to now consider this Seventh Plane as the First Plane of Evolution in Descension within The Oneness. In a time, long ago, not conceived as time, the evolvement of energy into various forms was stimulated by a need to understand the importance of an existence. In other words, we were explorers seeking a purpose just like you. As we subdivided, creating more forms out of the ethers of The Oneness, we became conscious of a need to control our explorations. This instinctive inbuilt need to control is, and will always be, a direct encoded sublime truth that we are all a part of the Primal Fragment. We were the first to awaken to substance, need, and expansion without judgment or decisions being made. Subsequently, all forms that we shall now call entities, were given the freedom to explore too. In truth, we are all still exploring and will continue to do so forever more!

So when you consider that the First Plane of Spiritual Evolution was in existence, you might imagine yourself as a supremely powerful entity with a very wise Old Soul memory. Unfortunately, that is not the case. As was stated earlier, confusion and chaos arose, causing The Oneness to lose its balance, while the purpose of existence was lost. Entities took on all types of forms, some considered hideous, while other were defined as beautiful. Today, in your time, we are still recovering Entities long lost in the ways of earthly beliefs, who are either disruptive and malefic to Humans or who play paranormal tricks with anyone or anything, while generating negative energy to create chaos for those Humans and animals who appear to be a reflection of their dark source. We shall say of this source, that it is of the nature of the Dark Side before The Oneness was ever truly known to exist within each of us. During our period of awakening, The Oneness was beyond our consciousness of understanding in what we were to become. In other words, like babies, we had to grow up and assume responsibility for all we had created. Hence the reason, that stirs us on to find those Entities that are alone and seemingly forgotten.

Entities can be only of The Dark, who are our opposing selves, mirrored from the days of our own darkness. Yes, there are Archangels of The Dark too! They oversee the balance of the First and Second Planes of Evolution in Ascension. Their ways are hard and often very aggressive, establishing a survival nature in each newborn Fragment. Their Chief Features being the coding they enacted upon, as was explained earlier in this text. Some Spiritual Fragments now incarnated, are able to integrate with them, depending on their own Soul Group and Master Teachers who work with them, to off-set the balance of the Higher Arche.

The see-saw of this balance is ever evolving. On Earth, looking back over your history, you are able to see an enormous amount of spiritual growth, in spite of the interference of The Dark Side of your encoded nature. No fragment can incarnate without some aspects of The Dark Side being active. Remember, from your earlier forms of life, you have learned to become aware of the way you interact with others, in ways that teach you a great deal more about The Oneness. It is because of your incarnated existences, that we work so diligently to keep the balance of The Oneness within you, by stimulating your modes of action or, perhaps possibly, help you to change you point of view, while you are asleep!

On this First Plane of Evolution, Fragments focus on existence in destruction, where there is only the joy of making and breaking self in a variety of forms. The concept of self is individual in each form with free will, yet equal to one another when united. On the Seventh Level of this First Plane of Evolution, there is only an innate acceptance of their existence encoded in the mirror image of the First Plane of Creation, where the First Primal Fragment created self within the Dark Side. In the act of creation, the light was born. Friction within the separation of the Higher and Lower aspects of the Primal Fragment was awakened to growth. You can now see the necessity for spiritual growth, which provides a polarity of Dark and Light, versus Light and Dark, both being vitally important to the existence of The Primal Fragment.

Understand that each level in this Higher Plane of Descension has a direct hold on the equivalent Lower First Plane of Form that is in Ascension. Here we see the entwining layers of all levels, whether in opposition or support, functioning actively in Descension or Ascension, to be constantly active in keeping The Oneness alive and well for all Fragments that exist on all forty-nine levels.

To make things clearer, imagine you are the first human to exist, and discover you have a talent to make something else out of yourself. So, you meditate and awaken to your energy vibrations and oscillate at a frequency that simulates a part of your energy to take on a new form, making a toy for you to play with. Once you have explored it, and know it well, you become bored with your toy and toss it away, where it lays until it too can generate its own energy, and once again stimulates self to act in form. So the journey never ends. Each Fragment can create all manner of forms in any life lived. Today in your world, you make objects to play with. An ability to modulate and control sound into form has long been lost! However nothing lost is forgotten!

The First Plane of Evolution struggled to find its own self-control. Within those struggles, our consciousness of emotion was stimulated to grow and evolve, giving us Divine Purpose, some rules, and regulations with regard to reincarnation of all Fragments. Hence the Laws of Karma explained earlier. On Earth, you may think those Laws of Karma do not apply! On the contrary, they are so deeply embedded within your coding, that you cannot knowingly shut them out, since the *Chief Features* will return you to contemplate your *Soul Structure Coding* and to investigate your spiritual *Attitude*. These laws and your coding entwine in every life you have lived and when in between lives, they directly assist you in your journey towards the next step in evolution.

We Archangels, having been given the freedom to explore, are now returning to The Oneness to refresh our long period of overseeing your growth. We thank you for all that you have done but must concede that without your transitions that are occurring now, we would not be able to refresh ourselves. We will remind you that what occurs in the Seventh Plane of Evolution, is a direct emanation of The Prime Directive of the Prime Fragment. We are all simply aspects of its creation and its continuance. In that sense, every Fragment, whether incarnated or existing on any of the forty-nine levels, has a choice and the freedom to act. When one Fragment responds, the whole is shifted to adapt and reunite in a new form of understanding and creation.

Our return to the Seventh Level in Ascension will require us to upload all our experiences to The Prime Fragment, who in receiving us, will absorb, absolve and re-orient self to awaken to a new lesson to be shared among all Fragments. Thus a new *Age of Enlightenment* is given to all. As a result, we will all shift our points of view, bond in various other ways, and then as is deemed appropriate, will amalgamate our new intentions into new Soul Groups that unify within the heart of Love Divine and all Fragments of The Oneness.

As we amalgamate and integrate upon our return to The Oneness of the seventh level in the Seventh Plane, we will re-purpose our connections with all and correlate the new lessons into our new forms, that will be shared with Humans when the timing is right. When you look back in your history, you will notice that many angelic appearances were recorded during times of change. It will be no different this time. You will be awakened with new understandings of your own spiritual journey and your purpose in being incarnated at this time, and on during the next few hundred years to come.

All that has occurred in The Piscean Age will be filtered, assimilated, and sorted into new categories of learning, just as the previous Ages of the past have been absorbed and understood as self-explained in all Fragments. When relative to an earthly situation where instinct kicks in, there awakens within the deep-subconscious the 'Knowing Self,' will instantly arise. Every Human will recall information, together with emotions to make a choice. Then to act upon that choice, while beginning to live a purposeful life.

In this new early period of The Great Aquarian Age, you will be proud to be educated and useful in a variety of ways, having been stimulated by the new Soul Groups that will meld mentally with you all as was promised. You can expect a great deal of negative energy being discharged from each Fragment incarnated. Yes, when Humans need to change, they become destructive, just like the upper echelons did so very long ago, now called the Seventh Plane of Evolution. Our early chaos is still encoded and seen when Humans, who are out of balance, cause various issues on a daily basis.

As we descend from the forty-nineth Level, to the forty-eighth, and so on, we will awaken new ways to exist within our world and that of your Earth. Always remember the *Forth Karmic Law*, reminds you that you are always a mirror-image of those you encounter on any level of existence. Since like attracts like, you will never be alone! Your spiritual awareness of our forms will amplify your wisdom, but you may well find yourself physically alone frequently. Knowing how to function alone will be a new lesson for you all to understand how the inner workings of your mind, your status, and your spiritual awakening combined, will lead you to function in a different way, thus providing you with a golden opportunity to evolve in creating new ways to live on Earth.

As The First Plane of Evolution in Descension restructures its form, the levels within it will adapt, sending energy signals to all that lies within The Oneness. A new beginning in the beliefs of leadership with empowerment, blessed by The Oneness, will evolve on Earth. This new belief in each Fragment's need to evolve spiritually, will become vital to all that incarnate. The spiritual nature of Mankind will also evolve to mirror image our unity of this First Plane of Descension. You will seek ways to find peace, listen and learn. In time, your world will become a school of enlightenment for all levels within The Planes of Evolution. You will receive a new wave of differently encoded Fragments, who are in Descension. These are the wisest of The Oneness who will incarnate in leadership to aid the creation of new structures, suggesting new ways and means to exist. This occurrence is vital for 'The Shift,' so named by your all on Earth, to start the process of awakening a new lesson for all. That lesson is Harmony!

Now, let us explain that the Sixth Level of Ascension is now called the Second Level of Descension where creative existence will set the pace for Descension. Here, The Ascended Masters will make plans to appear in human forms, being temporarily very physical, in a variety of ways, in order to connect with individuals in person. Of course, this journey was pre-arranges long ago before the Fragment (Spirit) is incarnated. Each of these specially chosen incarnated Spirits can recall with his/her psychic senses, the commitment made as a Fragment of The Oneness, and immediately responds with love and trust. On Earth, their conversations will influence one another, to ensure there is an awakening of awareness in establishing self-will, to define their united spirituality and philosophy with regard to hopes and dreams.

When a physical connection is made by The Ascended Master with an incarnated Fragment, their Spirits will entwine in love and a sharing of information. Then when the message is received, The Ascended Master will usually, suddenly disappear into a crowd or be gone instantly when you turn your back. Upon returning to The Oneness, The Ascended Master is heavy with energy absorbed from Earth. His or Her Spiritual energy is relayed to all other Fragments in ascension on the Sixth Level of The Seventh Plane of Evolution, while also integrating the same information to Masters in Descension on what is now called the lower Second Level of Descension. Though this Plane is in harmony with The Oneness, all Fragments still being entwined, those descending, commit to taking their first step in separation, using the Primal *Goal of Submission* in complete *devotion (The Light)* and its opposite *subservience (The Dark)*. So the transformation begins. A great deal of dormant negativity that the Ascended Masters have been absorbing and processing is now shared with the Descending Masters who will then descend to the

Fifth Level where preparation is made to journey through the lower levels of the Seventh Plane and on to the Sixth Plane of Evolution to process the human form to be taken. A Descending Master has a choice of millions to choose from. and on down to the Astral Levels of The Forth Plane of Evolution. In this way, by passing through each Plane of Evolution, the Descending Masters are prepared for life on Earth.

Before descending through the lower Levels of this Sixth Plane of Evolution, these Great Masters will absorb more negativity, knowing they will need to use it while in temporary Human form. They each combine their energies as a Soul Group Incarnate, shifting energies back and forth, absorbing new input, while discarding the old. Their temporary physical forms and connections these Descended Masters take will be prepared in The Upper Astral, where they will make a strong spiritual connection with the incarnated Spirit they are about to help.

Once the connection is made and information shared, the now Descended Master Teacher will return to the Upper Astral knowing that his Human student will not only remember his/her visit, but will share, even teach others, across the world. In The Upper Astral, the Master Teacher will maintain contact spiritually with their student Human until they pass back into The Astral Plane of their spiritual coding. Once all is balanced, The Descended Master may return to their own Plane of Evolution. In this scenario, The Ascended Master Teacher returns to the Seventh Plane of Evolution where they resume their true vibration. However, their return to the Seventh Plane of Evolution creates changes that, until that instant, would be unknown.

In order to make this very important spiritual connection with a Human on Earth, The Descended Master Teacher has knowingly absorbed some of the Darkness of Earth, bringing it back, first to The Upper Astral and then on to the Second Level of Descension in the Seventh Plane of Evolution. This Seventh Plane of Evolution is constantly transforming as a result of changes made in the Ascending and Descending Fragments. Such is the mirror-image of the beginning of your awakening to the idea of 'The Shift' in consciousness that actually began in 2008. Some incarnated Fragments are the fore-runners of what is to occur, so heed their warnings!

Various types of spiritual encounters will also be a test for the Descending Spirit Fragment (*Master Guide)* who must now embrace earthly ways while in contact with a Fragment (*Human)*. This wise Ascended Master has become a Master Guide to embrace and share all the pain and suffering that has gone before in Ages past and also feels what is happening to those living on Earth. In sharing this earthly emotional and mental state, the Collective Ascended Ones, on the Seventh Plane of Evolution, each have their own identical awakening in knowing how the various states of discord on Earth, are being played out. They are of one mind, one heart, and one Soul. These physical insights into human existence, never experienced by these Primary Fragments before, becomes the foundation stone upon which to generate a new source of energy. That encoded energy will then be passed down through all Levels by Fragments in Descension. In the release and manifestation of this encoded energy, a new slant in the approach to understanding wisdom is awakened in Mankind. This act of Divine intervention is relative to the lessons learned in Ages past. These great Ascended Masters have a purpose; to sow seeds of enlightenment, as time passes in your world. New concepts of existence will later emerge.

As Ascended Fragments from the Third Level of The Third Plane of Evolution incarnate, they will be born into flesh for very short periods of time, when Divine Love will flow through them, offering insights channeled from the wisdom of Divine Consciousness. Out of the mouths of babes will come the messages of peace and love.

As the evolved Descending Fragments unify with Ascending Fragments, such unity in understanding both The Dark and The Light causes changes instantly. The moment these Fragments merge, changes in the mirror-image of the Seventh Plane of Ascension occur on Earth at the same time. On Earth you act out our spiritual conflict, giving us insight into the need for re-organization, to achieve balance and harmony on all forty-nine levels. When friction is in harmony, musical notes abound. Actions create reactions. The Force of The Oneness is fully felt by all Fragments in any of the Seven Planes of Evolution. On Earth you reflect this imbalance constantly, since you are all trained to judge and condemn. As you battle your way through life, conflict becomes a daily issue.

The messages that Ascended Masters bring to your world is consistently the same. To love one another despite the many differences you see in yourself and in your life's circumstances. Your decisions, the way you act in behavior, also your beliefs and habits, are our lessons too. Everything you are today has been shared spiritually with us and other Humans who will continue to evolve quite naturally on Earth. In your future, emphasis will be laid on education and unification of your species. Each incarnated Fragment will seek equality of the various different races that share your world. Animals will become more docile and appreciative of their existence too. We could say of your humanism, that you are becoming lightworkers, each encoded with a new primal coding to evolve your species. All these changes on Earth are being directed by the Ascending and Descending Fragments of the Seventh Plane of Evolution, here referred to as the First Plane of Descension.

As eons of time pass in your world, your encounters with incarnated Fragments from what was the Sixth Plane of

Ascending Fragments, will now be the new Plane of Evolution, generally known as the new Second Plane of Descension. This pattern will continue on down through all Planes. The First Dark Plane of Evolution will become the last Plane of Descension. Here new forms of energy will create new patterns that will be resonating in a new frequency, thus allowing a bonding between the birthing of new Souls who will in the future of Earth and other realms be stimulated to ascend into physical forms in various states of awareness, with separate causes and challenges not seen before. Your bio-genetically engineered form will change as you adapt to the changes Mother Earth will force upon you.

This transformation of form on all forty-nine levels will bring about a great spiritual change in the unification and values of all Fragments on all *Levels of Existence*, who now fully understand that each is responsible for all it/you creates on every Level. No longer will Levels be structured and type cast. Each Level will be a time of unity for all Fragments, whether incarnated or not! If we itemize it according to your perceptions now. A foe is a friend and a friend is an enemy. How then shall you know yourself. Are you a friend or a foe? Will you disturb *The Force* of the flow of The Oneness, or will you support it by embellishing it?

We can see here, quite easily, that those at the top of the tree will exchange places with those at the roots of the tree! The question remains, allowing for free will of all Fragments, how this new plan will evolve in ways that make life on any planet more harmonious to all living things wherever they may be? How will all incarnating Descending Ancient Elders achieve spiritual transformation in The Dark Side of The Oneness and in each person born on Earth? As you say, "What will be, will be!" Freedom allows every Spirit within a Fragment to have choice at all times, on all forty-nine levels. This will bring a surprising change in The Cosmos.

Of course, this plan will take thousands of years to manifest forms and new existences in places you cannot image now. But, let us not forget that imagination is the essential tool for creating something that is conducive to the change. Each Fragment, whether an Ascended Master or a new born Soul will, in some way, unify and create a better world(s) for all Fragments to play in.

So what of the Ascended Soul Groups that act as an anchor for The Oneness to continue adapting? It is known, on Earth, that when a new enterprise begins, people suddenly appear interested and soon many gather together to find new ways and means to integrate business, and pleasure in some way that will benefit Mankind. When we see how well incarnated Fragments integrate, whether it be in states of controversy or agreement, there is always a great change in societies and their general points of view. People who are out of date, tied to old ways, leave, while young ones take their place, bringing new ideas. While they suggest new approaches to dealing with issues, they will be implanting, and developing new rules that others will follow. It is no different for the Descending Ascended Souls as they incarnate. They will be leaders who will bring great changes.

Since these Old Soul Groups are now in Descension and will incarnate, new Soul Groups will evolve from the Ascending Fragments on the Fifth & Six Planes of Evolution. This new unity will be founded on old incarnated experiences that will be assimilated and then deprogrammed. Once history is mastered in The Spiritual Consciousness of all who come together, a ceremonial bonding occurs that allows the forming of a new *Upper Arche,* collectively known as The Holy Spirit or The Brotherhood. With a grand assortment of great newly Ascended Masters, who have collectively become the Master Soul Group. They will create a new beginning for all. This new Master Soul Group will have taken gentle control over time, and who have also created smaller Soul Groups on all levels of all Planes. This Plan will support all Fragments in all forms of life whether in The Oneness or on planets throughout the Cosmos.

Since I, Haniel and my brothers are given the task of creation and unification of all Fragments, we are now making ourselves available to talk with any Fragment who seeks our assistance and advice. In the past, we have remained more distant, but now through this new Age of Enlightenment when all Fragments are awakened to our presence, then we are made communal in all things made form. Our journey of creation has taken us through Eons of Ages and, as has been plainly seen, involved great pain, suffering and disassociation from The Oneness. Here it should be known and accepted, that we the creators of human form are now a known part of each Fragment, and therefore, available to integrate our wisdom with those who ask for help.

You have waited a long time for the Age of Enlightenment, and now it is upon you. Make ready within and we will succor you wholly. For the blessings of one is for all. Be the key to our future! Create and enjoy the newness of all that is! Ultimately, the lesson for all is to walk the Middle Road. Some may say they already walk in the way of The Enlightened Buddha where all things are neutral. We firmly remind you that all in The Oneness is felt, therefore, there is no true neutral form of existence where nothing matters but spirituality, and peace, in just existing. One would miss the joy of perception and creation.

Authors note: Journey Into An Unknown World: The Way To Oneness Revisited will explain more and is available on amazon.com as softback and eBook.

CHAPTER NINE
Acceptance: The Road Where The Dark & Light Sides Meet.

Throughout this book, thus far, we have talked about the importance of Divine Friction that enables The Oneness to continue indefinitely. The concept of a new beginning is almost like saying we are closing down to start afresh. However, that is not the case as explained earlier in this book. But, because of the awakening of a new Age of Enlightenment, there must be some aspects of form that are in agreement, where there is no friction. This of itself, will slow down the pace of change.

In comparisons with bi-gone Ages where there was less activity to become involved in, your generations and those who bore you are in fact, stressed, overworked, under-paid and so forth, as a result of perhaps too much involvement. Yet, despite all this, the Age of Technology has filled your hours with activities that give little time for fun and pleasure. We are happy to inform you that, though technology is here to stay, it will become easier for some when new apps are created. Others will still depend on older ways of communication while awaken their Soul Structure Codings to create an alternative method, where sound becomes the all-out new way to use energy, providing heat, power, comfort, and good health in a variety of ways not yet understood. Here in this chapter, we intend to explain some of the new ways that will evolve from friction created by unheard sounds!

There are many forms of sound that surround your world! Most of which you do not hear, since human range of hearing is limited. It was limited for a reason! Too much sound coming from The Oneness would drive each of you insane. Therefore, as we speak about the new awakening of sound in technology, we warn you to be careful! Too much resonation of sound can misalign your body, mind, and emotions, causing your Spirit to crumble under the weight of change.

When we gave Crystal Acupuncture & Teragram Therapy to Dr. Margaret, she was unaware of sound coming from her stones that she used. When she was a small child, certain stones seemed to speak to her. In her mind it said, "Take me home!" What she was really hearing was a noise some kilohertz out of her hearing, but which made her feel relaxed and more at ease. As she grew up, this love of stones led her to create her healing modalities with our and various other Master Teachers to awaken her to the essential form of sound.

When you hold a stone in your hand, you hold something that vibrates energy and you feel it. What you feel is your own energy pulsating through the stone, which in turn, becomes overloaded with energy as it tries to pass through, and around molecules within the stone. In an ultimate mini explosion, the stone disperses light into your hand and suddenly that light travels through your Five Bodies: Physical, Etheric, Spirit, Higher Mind and Soul, regenerating them as blocks of energy are dispersed from the Aura. This simple act of attuning to a stone has freed you from negativity you have held on to. That negativity is relative to the RNA that you have absorbed from others within your family and outer circles of associates. This simple explanation is equal to and both the same and yet, different throughout The Oneness.

No matter what Plane of Evolution a Fragment is on, there is always a personal transition between creation and destruction. In every case when a Fragment releases history and awakens to new information, there is an ascension in self. Should you be in a negative state, then the reverse is seen. Controversy creates friction. Part of you wants to be right and part of you wants to be wrong. This dichotomy creates friction on a daily basis within your Aura. If you adapt, and embrace this concept given from the Seven Planes of Evolution, you will see the dichotomy between them all. Some are Ascending, while others are Descending Fragments. By passing by or interacting with one another in any way, they will create a ripple sound throughout The Oneness. We wish you to understand this simply. As you held a stone in your hand and felt a change in you, so it will be in any of the Planes. Each Fragment is vital to The Oneness in that their force of life matters.

When your body functions, you are actively creating sound, even when sleeping. Your particular resonation can be felt by a psychic, a healer, a teacher, and anyone in The Oneness, who are of The Dark or of The Light. When you psychologically become bad tempered and animated, you generate a great deal of negative energy. That energy feeds back into the earth, the walls, other people present, and so much more. You may be thinking of years past, even recreating patterns of existence from old ancestors who have returned to the Oneness in The Astral. Every sound you make verbally, or words you think in your mind become signals sent outward from your body, in the hope of connecting with someone somewhere in time! We wish you to understand that your resonation is important not only for you to seek company, but also for us in The Oneness to help you. Remember, we cannot help you under the first Law Of Karma; you must ask for help!

Acceptance of all that is can sound ominous to a negative mind, while the alternative to a positive mind, could be overwhelming. Imagination will often send you spinning in the wrong direction, ending up with misery and despair. Or, conversely, enjoy a great event that occurs which can leave you with energy wasted, and a desire manifested to move on. You can see here that involvement in the transformation of the Oneness must set every fragment into a sensed awareness of protection in survival. It is no different in The Oneness when Descending

Older Souls, pass by younger Ascending Souls who are transforming and adapting to the entire energy force-field of The Oneness. In simple terms, they are changing the way energy has been enmeshed. This unscrambling of the past is frightening and yet stimulating to all Fragments on every Level, in every Plane of Evolution. Hope abounds for a new and better world to live in, be it the Spirit World or your earthly one.

Part of our new journey into the unknown, is the ability to accept change as immediate and a test. That which works will unfold new actions and new ways and means, while if it fails, the test will give birth to new ideas. Every idea is a generated sound that emanates across The Oneness and across all forms of life. To enter a New Age, is to learn to accept new lessons, new forms of productivity, with many new and strange varieties of performance. Each performance creates even more energy as you fail or succeed.

Your planet is very noisy within its core and is in sync with the Oneness. As The Oneness transform, so your Planet Earth will too. Weather patterns will change, along with land masses and ocean floors causing great waves. Fear not of self-destruction, or annihilation of your species. Instead, prepare to transform yourself to a new age of awareness, and most importantly, be a part of the way sound will be used.

Into your world, will enter more advanced Souls who will bring wisdom in waves of energy to you all. From The Darkness of what was, you will arise as a more aware species, who will rebuild the world according to new rules, where all incarnated Fragments will have more action in their coding. This awakening will be brought about by new aspects of the DNA manifesting in your cells; reforming to transform your perception into a more sharing mode. In truth your bio-chemistry will be different. After all, you were made according to the now active Primal Fragment, who requires spiritual growth in order to remain The Prime

Fragment. Here we see the Dark & Light sides of The Oneness reflected in all Fragments which results in destruction first, followed by a planetary healing.

Because each of you is prone to expect the negative to occur, we first began to implement the Collective Soul Groups of animals to mingle by softening the hearts of animals. You will have noticed that the hunter will lie down with the hunted in a state of satisfaction through a bond of love. Birds play with cats. Lions with humans and so forth. In this way, each Human has been easily awakened to an awareness of Divine Love in these creatures. As you know, animals have been seen to actively save their owners when danger appears. Here we see not only love, but loyalty to a causal command from The Oneness; to give protection at all cost, even unto death! Therein lies a message of knowing that life continues after death, a reminder that each Fragment must return to The Astral.

So let us speak more about the importance of The Lower and Upper Levels of the Third and Forth Planes of Evolution. When a Fragment incarnates from the Fifth Level in the Third Plane Plain of Evolution, they have evolved enough, and are ready to explore life in Human form. These Fragments are primal in exploring and surviving, which while in action, generates more energy in sound to form musical notes. When life ends, they return to the Fifth Level from whence they came. While there again, they will find themselves wanting to know more about life and then stimulate a need to return to Earth. Fragments from the Forth Plane of Evolution, in the Upper Astral, will assist their return, ensuring that their Soul Structure Coding will inspire them to try a little harder to awaken while incarnated again. Time and time again they will be born, die and return until they are successful in acquiring a passion to evolve in awareness for a different purpose. By then, they each will have overcome their remembrances of being a Baby and later a Young Soul, that has

Ascended away from The Dark Side. They will have passed through the remaining two levels of The Third Plane of Evolution, having changed their energy many times in an evolved vibration that resonates balance. Then the real fun begins! They have found the musical key of C Major, where all forms begin to Ascend in vibration. Here we should explain that all forty-nine levels oscillate at their own separated vibration, which when balanced will create a melody throughout The Cosmos and The Oneness.

Incarnating Fragments from the First Level of the Fourth Plane of Evolution will incarnate on Earth as newly refreshed Mature Souls who are now considered to be on a journey of Ascension from The Dark Side, to now embrace The Light Side. Each Fragment is now awakened to the importance of making another equally long journey, in a continued stream of lives to be lived on the physical Plane of Earth. Each must pass through the seven materially oriented Levels of Existence under the influence of Earth's emanation. Each Fragment, now called a Spirit in embodiment, will suffer, and learn in many ways until they evolve to enter The Fifth Plane of Evolution. The Forth Plane of Evolution, is both The Earth and The Lower & Upper Astral Levels in the Spirit World, known by Humans as Hell and Heaven.

Know that, time after time, you and your Collective Soul Group have and will continue to incarnate with a purpose. That purpose is to use enlightened consciousness in Human form. When a collective Soul Group incarnate across your planet, you may never know them physically, but will feel them and respond in kind to the situation that calls for unity of the many incarnated Fragments, who wish to make a stand for something that is truly important to their well-being, and that of The Oneness. Earth is the battle ground where the Dark Force of nature entwines with the Light force of The Oneness. Memories will be stimulated, allowing all incarnated Fragments to awaken and recall Past Lives and the lessons learned, where relative, to ensure a positive action in the current life lived.

We should point out here, that Soul Groups often incarnate with a Soul Group plan of action. Each Fragment within the group is encoded with a Goal of Growth, where negative versus positive happenings will test all emotions, in order to find trust in self, and a belief in The Oneness, you call God. As you know, it is not unusual to pray to God in your world. When a Fragment is in prayer, a sense of belonging occurs, even if nothing physical happens to prevent their worst fears manifesting as a test.

Many fears you have experienced in Past Lives and now in the past, are overcome from life to life. Here we need to remind you that as below, so above is true. We fear annihilation that could manifest, in a form of collapse, where all Fragments are scattered with no sense of unity in Oneness or remembrance of The Prime Fragment. Your World Wars have often threatened the balance of this unity and the harmony of all life forms throughout all Planes of Evolution. Yet, in spite of this spiritual fear, The Creator, our Prime Fragment, has always found a way to harmonize and unify all excess energy through absorption, which is then neutralized and returned as a gift of healing throughout The Oneness, reminding all Fragments that God, the Prime Fragment is supreme and in awareness of all that is.

As each Fragment dies, leaving their body in Spirit form, it always returns to The Plane from whence it came. On arrival, this Spirit will celebrate its return by joining in harmony with all other Fragments that have been entwined within his/her past life just completed. Enemies are once again friends. Master Spirit Guides and Teachers are always available in the Upper and Lower Astral Planes. These teachers will lead the newly arrived Spirit to observe their last life in the Halls of Learning that exist in The

Astral of the Level they belong to. There are many Halls of Learning on each Level to be explored. By the time the incarnated Fragment has returned many times, they have become aware of their own Ascension and choose whether to return to Earth or move on to the final Seventh Level, in preparation for unity and acceptance in joining with the Fifth Plane of Evolution.

With the years passing and Fragments, now called Spirits, continually reincarnating, a spiritual sense of awareness has now awakened in you all. You no longer live to face death and return to The Planes of Evolution, but instead yearn to bring your Spiritual side of self into the forefront of evolvement. You are all on a journey home. In time we will all be part of The Prime Fragment, who will in further time, manifest a new world with new forms in a new Universe. This upheaval and change is not imminent in your time. Nor is time truly a word for the measurement of the evolvement of The Prime Fragment. All time is now and will always be now. What was in your world is history, yet in our consciousness in The Astral and Upper Planes, all is happening now. What is to come, is the unknown, much of which is unknowable to you now.

Outside influence can occur, such as the meeting of interplanetary species. Though The Oneness will not interfere, we watch closely. We learn from your experiences and formulate new dynamics in entwining not only Universes, but also Galactic consciousness of all species ever created. Each Universe has its Fragments. Fragments can evolve and begin afresh, by incarnating into a new form of life and living, somewhere far away from Planet Earth. Since this news takes you into a complicated imaginative situation, you can become confused. There is a great awakening now of life forms on other planets, and many incarnated Fragments on your Planet are remembering close encounters of a first kind. Contact!

Since the Oneness has many facets of creation, this becomes too involved for you to understand. It is sufficient to say that some of you are awakening to Past Lives lived on other Planets, not in your Solar System, or have visited Earth in very ancient times, as makers and creators of new Universes. Yes, you must remember, that many Fragments who are Ascended, can incarnate anywhere. Some choose to awaken those past lives as a doorway to Universal consciousness where all things are known. Yet, when in the flesh, few can recall much, since too much information can become destructive. Fear can become rampant, and the death toll high.

Such destructive forms of action would not serve The Oneness well. If an event should occur, where all things made are likely to be used in destruction, there would be a cosmic reaction. Some speak of a Galaxy, the hub of unification for all Galactic species to congregate. It is assumed that those who dwell there are fully aware, not only of their own species, but also in the knowing that Planet Earth is prime property to be conquered. Many of you erroneously believe they will use all their destructive forces to mirror-image The Prime Fragment, in becoming the Prime Leaders of Universes. As you now know, this kind of leadership is destructive not only to all forms of life, but to The Oneness too. So, to prevent invasion, we the Archangels and those of the Brotherhood do not allow Fragments to cross space and time yet! No one is ready for this type of invasion. You are ready for the occasional contact that has been going on for many centuries. There are three species that have integrated themselves with you. They are The Sheezeetah, The Arcturians and the Lirians; Ancient Fragments, who are encoded to entwine themselves as teachers in your world.

All other forms you talk about are in existence, but not enhancing your world for the betterment of you all. They are worrisome, but that is all. They will test your spirituality in many ways. Often, your dreams allow access, when you cross the vast space of Universes to awaken telepathically to other species. When you become conscious, you must understand and remember that the Spirit of each Fragment is still the form by which we travel from place to place in an instant. If you dream of being with Aliens, then in a Spirit sense, you probably have.

Here we should refer to the balance of The Cosmos. It is vast, beyond your understanding, yet within this vastness is the evolution of energy. Energy turns into matter where forms manifest out of The Ethers of The Oneness. In some senses, this manifestation of new forms is expected, yet when it happens, most are amazed and perhaps afraid. As you watch your sky at night, you look for more Planets. The '*Seeding of Planets*' takes eons of Universal Time when cosmic energy disperses, leading to its own reseeding, time and time, again.

Within The Cosmos, are energies that form patterns that you may define as mathematical in forms, such as triangles, cubes, and circles. We will not deny this perception, but rather encourage you to understand through the science of sound, how all things have shape, structure, and resonation. One could say of The Cosmos, that the echoing sounds play a wonderful melody for all to hear. Unfortunately, this Melody is blocked by dense energy created by you all, since you still exist in negativity. You all gather together in fear, mirror-imaged, time and time again, for all people on Earth to learn and awaken to sharing, as each Era ended. Your pathways have all been filled with experiences that have taught you to question your existence. Each one of you searches for inner peace, yet the conflict of all that you have learned from your peers, has by your own choice, set you on a pathway of exploration to find a value in attaining inner peace.

Since the Goal of Acceptance is the Prime Fragment's Soul Coding, it is essential that all other Fragments integrate within their Spirit essence, acknowledging the God-like self! By sensing a connection with the inner calling of acceptance in transition, whether in Ascension or Descension, a Spirit Entity can adapt accordingly to any needed lessons, by being provided a connection through experiences in becoming a part of the Universal balance of your Solar System. In an earthly sense, your interest in the Solar Systems, Astrology and Astronomy, has revealed new ideas associated with space exploration. In times yet to come, once again, your species will take journeying to the stars seriously, but not before new technology is given from The Oneness as befits the times of transition into a new Universal Consciousness, where more can be revealed, relative to those times yet to come.

The entwinement of each Fragment is highly interactive and very important to the patterns of existence that bind you all to The Oneness. In the following chapter we will address this complicated overlap of the Third, Fourth and Fifth Planes of evolution.

CHAPTER TEN
Assimilation Of The Third, Forth & Fifth Planes Where Discord Leads To Harmony.

The Third, Forth & Fifth Planes of Evolution are where Fragments in discord learn to embrace spiritual harmony. A Fragment is now almost constantly in a Spirit form, whether in The Lower or Upper Astral or, of course, incarnated on Earth. When a person dies, their Spirit leaves their body, releasing all forms of mental and emotional entrapment. Instantly, they instinctively return to their Level in their Plane of Evolution. They immediately congregate with other Spirits who welcome them to explore and examine one's self-perceptions without judgment. A clear perception of self is the ideal

From our point of view, assimilation is to understand, know and use all aspects of emotional expression when each Fragment returns to The Astral. There we share in their spiritual growth as they integrate their experiences to bind us all, in an ever-evolving pattern of spiritual and physical growth. There never has been judgment or disappointment, no matter the size, shape, or form that a Spirit incarnates with. Wherever they lived their lives, it provided an integration of actions, when energy was released for The Oneness to evolve. So let us define the nature of a Spirit.

Since the refined harmonious sound of resonance in the Upper Planes of Evolution is completely entwined for all Ascended Fragments that do not incarnate, you can begin to understand that those who take on a physical form, will need a spiritual form too. Those of us in the Fifth Plane's Upper Levels and above need no form. We are consciousness in an everlasting shifting energy form that frequently is retuned to the call of all Fragments. Each

Fragment, whether existing in the Upper Levels of the Third Plane of Evolution, *(Lower Astral)*, of The Dark Side, or Fragments from the First & Second Levels Of the Fifth Plane of Evolution, *(Upper Astral)*, of The Light Side, will be born in the flesh, with an intention in achieving Ascension. Meanwhile, those in The Light Side, who are focused on Descension and creation will interact within the levels of all three Planes of Evolution. In the following pages, we will explain how these interactions of Ascension and Descension are vital and necessary for the evolution of all that exists in The Oneness.

When a dark natured Spirit is ready to incarnate, they will find a Fragment that is more enlightened to become a Guardian Angel, Spirit Guide, and helper when they incarnate. The job of the more ascended Fragment is to nurture their association with the embodied Fragment by teaching them to learn to enjoy physical forms on Earth.

All incarnated Fragments from the Upper Levels of The Third Plane will rely heavily upon their own inspirations in accepting development instinctively. They each will follow their own Soul Structure Coding buried within their deep-subconscious. Sensing self as a survivor, they encode their brains with physical experiences that stimulate an awakening to their Spirit form within their human form. They each will incarnate many times. Sometimes hundreds of times, until a lesson is learned, ensuring that all aspects of life after life experiences while in Human form, are assimilated, thus becoming more spiritually aware.

The Ascended Fragment is constantly working with their student Fragment to stimulate an understanding of the purpose of his or her existence. A negative incarnated Fragment will focus on the point of being incarnated and, most importantly, in learning how to balance their thoughts. Thoughts are simple energy forms of emotions that are stored in the brain, where a constant battle thrives between their failures and successes. You might say, they spend a lot of time exploring, experiencing and often in confusion. These early lives lived, are so vital to the Primal Fragment. Every action causes a reaction! Every incarnated Fragment causes a shift on your Planet, which in turn, causes a shift in the ebb and flow of The Oneness.

As each Fragment, from The Third Plane of Evolution, incarnates over many centuries or longer, an awakening of experiences in bonding with other incarnated Fragments develops an emotional tie, that may well last throughout many lives. Bonded Fragments will, in time, become a Soul Group who incarnate together with a purpose. That is, one of change through transformation of consciousness, beliefs, and actions. Such an event is occurring on Planet Earth now. We see your fears, we understand you are partly wanting transformation, while actually resisting it. This is very normal for your species and exactly what is required for all to keep The Oneness active, which in turn, will also transform the entirety of The Oneness. By the time a Fragment has reached the Forth Plane of Evolution, there is within this Fragment, a love of beauty and a desire to find peace within self that always arises.

Earth is The Forth Plane of Evolution. Incarnating Fragments can either be in Descension or Ascension. By interacting on Earth, each Human will insist their way is the right way! Here we once again see controversy! Both Fragments, whether in Ascension or Descension, will bond and live together for more innovative reasons, which ultimately leads to understanding how love stimulates a need to unite in a common cause. If you take time to study your world, you will clearly see the Levels of Ascension and Descension occurring right next to you on a daily basis. In fact, it maybe your role to be the 'bad guy.'

Your physical world is structured with Seven Levels of Creation in form. The First Level is the Earth itself that nourishes all forms of life. While we will not go into this now, we will say that living in the flesh for the first time can be overwhelming for a Spirit Entity, no longer referred to as a Fragment of The Oneness. On Earth, you have identities and forms that are necessary for communication and interaction. So, let us look at the countries you see and their state of evolution whether in Descension or Ascension from The Oneness's point of view.

When you look at The Middle East, you see countries at war. You see destruction and desolation, starvation, and annihilation. This may look like Fragments from the Dark Side of life, who are now rising up to fight for their rights! What we see is the opposite! Fragments from The Fifth Plane of Evolution, now leaving their first and second levels, are incarnating Spirits who are descending to stir the process of your evolution up. For some it could be their very first time as a Spirit in a Human form. They may appear to be bad or good leaders. All that matters is that controversy moves the force of The Oneness to assimilate and rebalance.

As you ponder various lives of those living, you see countries where people are still native in mind, living on the land, completely unaware of your western technical world. Earth has worlds within worlds! Those worlds are levels of Ascension and Descension. Earth is the battle ground for all Fragments to incarnate, time and time again, as they each aspire to evolve one way or another. We also note that there are various demonstration of behavior, emotional responses, beliefs in various ways of existence, justified by circumstances. In every case, there is only a basic line that needs to be followed. Do what your instinct tells you to do to survive. So whether your story line is justified or not, is not our concern. What is our concern, is to nurture you through each lesson you personally create, by the way you process your thoughts and emotions. As teachers, we encourage, but never direct. Your free will is Divine Energy from The Prime Fragment. You are, therefore, stimulated to be active, even while sleeping.

Let us spend a moment here to consider how it must feel to meet an Ascended Master who is in human form, especially when a Fragment is extremely violent and hateful. They both seem to come from two separate states of awareness, so how can they bond? The Ascended Fragment is in a Descension Mode, incarnating to stimulate action and more awareness of The Oneness. By joining with this negative Fragment, the Ascended Fragment will entwine their ideas with a physical plan, which will in some way, introduce their negative incarnated student to think 'outside the box.'

Any slight change in outlook these two make, will stimulate physical emotional reactions, which will create a bigger change in awareness. Whatever they do together will affect many who hear about the pair. Together they walk side by side, until the plan of change is done. Their battles for the rights and wrongs of society may well call for desperate action, destruction, and violence, while for others, it could be the opposite. When two opposing views are brought together, there is always a challenge. Challenge is necessary if emotions are to be stimulated. Emotions carry the inner senses of the Divine Prime Fragment.

Human emotions vary immensely. Causes for emotional events to arise are always manifesting every second you breathe. New ideas fall from your brains, while new friends arrive to help you with your ideas. With determination arising out of necessity, each will pull aspects from their Soul Structure Coding, to develop various personalities traits, which will ensure a connection is made with other Fragments, who are synced together for a common event or cause. Many public events stimulate both the minority and majority of Fragments incarnated at this time on Earth. When a crowd bonds together in a common cause, you may think they are of like minds. This is not so! Some are here to tear down the old ways, while others are here to build anew. Yet still others require a mixture of both the old and the new. Those who are the rebels are the catalyst to change. Usually, they stand alone, with followers who add weight to their message. In every situation you can recall, you will always find controversy. In controversy, you will find very old and very immature souls united in a common goal. Change! Change occurs when Ascended Souls entwine themselves with Young Souls who are eager to invite change. On Earth, you see education, we see transformations and shifts in energy that better serves The Oneness.

When Fragments from the Third and Fifth Planes of Evolution unite on Earth in a common goal, The Forth Plane of Evolution, (*Earth,)* we see great spurts of growth followed by times of lack. This cycle of growth and destruction seen in so many different ways, too many to mention here, are vital to each life and the existence of Earth to continue in your Solar system. Once again, we remind you that all forms return to The Astral Planes that are the Etheric vibrations of all lives lived throughout all Eras. These records of assimilation, called The Akashic Records, are available to all Fragments whether incarnated or not. The Spirit of a Human is pure Divine energy that gives life to all. We say pure, in that its form is perfect for the Divine Focus of Change and Evolution on all Planes throughout all Levels therein. So, next time you want to fight with your friend, ask yourself. "Am I the Ascending or Descending Fragment in this situation?" You may be very surprised at your own answer. It is not unusual for an Ascending Fragment to incarnate and to feel they are negative and losing control of life. Well, they are, in order to do what they have come to do. Usually these bad choices and subsequent actions are a wake-up call to all those who have become settled and lack inspiration to aspire to greatness.

If a Fragment from The Third Plane of Evolution is interactive with a Fragment from The Fifth Plane of Evolution, while bonding on a spiritual level, they will unite in a common cause to awaken others to the rights and wrongs of life. So how will you know who is ascending versus, those descending? The answer is simple! Look for the way they encompass the light or the dark energy of a life. Look behind the masks they wear to see who this Spirit incarnated with you, truly is. When an Ascended Master is in embodiment, you can feel their power and dedication to help the world transform. Usually, they leave after they have done what was meant to be done. You have the memory of great Sages who have left valuable information on a variety of topics, that have led you to this time of change.

Since Earth has seven levels of existence, much of which you probably have never thought about, let us color this idea for you:

The North & South Poles - 1st Level where form is tested.
The Deserts   - 2nd Level where form awakens to life
The Oceans & Rivers   - 3rd Level of emotional awakening
The Swamps & Jungles   - 4th Level of survival and strength
The Fertile Land   - 5th Level of growth & sharing
The Cities   - 6th Level of spiritual tests
The Mountains   - 7th Level of release and awakening.

Living a life in just one of these places brings a person to understand they must be motivated in various ways to survive. As each struggles to survive, lessons are learned. Every life is full of lessons. When a life is ended they will return to the Lower or Upper Astral to reflect and awaken to further ways to share energy in another life. We can say that life after life is the building blocks of evolution for all that exists in The Oneness. Incarnations give all Fragments wonderful opportunities to flit from one place on Earth to another. You migrate and settle and move on frequently in a variety of ways. Your physical lives are your ascension in progress.

When you contemplate living in any one of the above places, you will quickly see in your now-time, how so many people congregate in various places to expand consciousness. Some travel far to find a new place to live, with hopes and dreams of happiness, only to find sorrow and misery. Perhaps you have a success story, where you made a fortune, yet are still miserable. Our point here is perspective. Life after life will give each of you a new perspective not only on your own life, but that of others. When you return to The Astral, you will assimilate the last life lived, with all other lives you have previously lived. You will also bond in assimilation with all friend's and foe's influences that have assisted you, to awaken to the importance of your part in The Oneness.

As Fragments descend and incarnate, passing time with Fragments that are ascending, one can find a very interesting point of reference. Old information is shared with any new information. Old emotions are rekindled to awaken old happenings for review. New emotions emerge as a 'light at the end of the tunnel,' which awakens something deep within the Spirit of a Human, who will immediately bond with anyone who appears supportive and connected to The Oneness. Whether that support is from The Dark Side or The Light Side is debatable in your world. Controversy is studied by all Fragments in The Oneness, since physical life causes stimulation, speculation of future happenings, that have potential growth for all Fragments, on all levels, in all The Planes of Evolution.

On Earth, rules and regulations abound. Freedom is taken from you. Choice seems to never be on the table. You feel controlled and tied down. Your Spirit feels restricted and lost. You are in the center of Earth's battles. You have fought your way up through the Lower three Levels of Earth's Planes of Evolution, having lived in The North & South Poles, The deserts, oceans, and rivers, swamps and in building and destroying cities to own land. All incarnations in the past have been negative and harmful. Out of pain came strength and resistance. The battle for existence was cruel and hard. However, the spiritual lessons were many and the result was a great shift in awareness and the value of life.

As your species evolved, many Ascended Fragments, now in Descension, incarnated to lead you towards embracing the light within the Upper Four Levels of The Astral. Many Humans are currently working through the Fifth and Sixth Levels of Earth to rebuild your homes, status, religions, philosophies and much more. With so much overcrowding and lack of support, many seek The Mountains, now known as the Seventh Level on Earth, where most, often escape the Sixth level of physical war to soothe their suffering, pain, and fear.

These seven physical Levels of your earthly Forth Plane of Evolution, allows you to live anywhere on your Planet. The result is an assortment of experiences that are contemplated within both the Lower and Upper Astral, often called The Spirit World. Spirits spend a great deal of time assimilating earthly mentality and emotions in all the many Halls of Learning upon their return. Once you have embraced all the Levels of Earth, now known as The Forth Plane of Evolution, you are ready for challenges. After your death, you will have arrived in the Upper Astral. There you will have awakened to the purpose of your existence in living in the Fourth or Fifth Levels of Earth, and in relating to your own spiritual evolution. In remembering and assimilating all that you have physically done to survive, you naturally evolve.

Remembering all aspects of Past Lives leads to an understanding of the importance of harmonizing all negative and positive emotional discords. Your Spirit has absorbed all your emotional drama from past lives lived in Ages long forgotten on Earth. Having incarnated hundreds of times on the first three Levels of Earth, where tribal groups lived and died, you learned to integrated your human species.

In modern times, you have incarnated on all seven Levels of Existence within the Forth Plane of Evolution, which we might add, is an exciting place to explore self. Never before have so many spiritual Fragments incarnated at the same time. Spirits from both the Lower & Upper Astral are uniting in a common cause to awaken unity, love, and harmony in the integration of your species. You can now freely choose where you want to live! You are now incarnated to embrace a spiritual knowing that your choice will manifest influences, that will stimulate others to make choices too! Will you choose the swamps, jungles, or fertile land to test your spiritual beliefs? We know some of the elders, still with you, will speak of lessons learned before technology!

When incarnated on the Forth and Firth Levels of Earth, you have accumulated a lot of information about Earth. Your levels of awareness begin to embrace a more spiritual point of view. You could be worshiping God or The Devil, whoever that may be, according to your own imagination. Imagination stimulates The Oneness to provide more support, education and to induce experiences that teach everyone to understand that all life matters. Wars have been fought over land. Land has become the hub of engineering and status. Financial chaos abounds! How then, will you find inner peace and the sanctity of love?

Your countries and cities are steeped in history. Yet at this time, you all turn your backs on those who broke down barriers in ways of their times. We say, here again, that no one incarnated Fragment has failed to enact out their role in the evolution of The Oneness. Understand that without those former pioneers, you would not be on Earth now. They each paved the way for your appearance on Earth. You could have been one of them in a past life too!

Your freedom to express yourselves in spirit, will, and culture, has offered you many ways to experience life on Earth. Yet, time and time again, what manifests must somehow be controlled by you all! We Ascended Masters cannot interfere. We cannot harm you or stop you from harming yourself. Life is precious in all forms of existence. Every Fragment is filled with love and healing, however low they fall. Each is a lesson to those they interact with. The good carries the bad, while the bad inspires the good. This continual ebb and flow is built into your nature. You will always be at odds with yourself. Your battle is between the dark and light of self. When you are in darkness you will seek the light. When the light is too much to bear, you will seek the dark. These reverse polarities are all over your Earth in all forms of life. Earth is the battle ground of The Oneness, where evolution begins and ends.

Each Fragment, incarnating with their Soul Structure Coding functioning, will also be carrying the DNA of ancestors, along with current RNA that is acquired from family and cultures etc., which pre-defines who you will become. What you each do within your nature will define your choices. You could become an Artisan, a Priest, a Scholar, a Kings, a Sage, a Warrior or even a Slave in the literal sense on Earth. This could even be the mirror-image of your Soul Archetype, where you truly test yourself against The Oneness. Here is our example: An Artisan Archetype decides to incarnate into a life as a talented artist who can play musical instruments, sing, and dance and paint too. While his or her life may sound spiritual with this coding, it is most likely to be hard since an Artist on Earth, must knock on every door to be seen and heard. The test in this case, could provide many situations where the incarnated Fragment interacts with the few or many, causing some kind of emotional response that once again gives life and energy to incarnated Fragments, who are looking for change.

If nothing else from this chapter, it is important to understand that no single Fragment is ever alone on any level or left unsupported. Everything you do on Earth in this Plane of Evolution is your golden opportunity to shine and rise up to the purpose of your life. Stand alone or with others and you will always aspire to be greater than you are.

Some might say that resistance is futile. We say that resistance is necessary on all levels of all Planes in Evolution. Remember every Fragment must assimilate all that has been experienced, both in the Dark and Light of all that is The Oneness. Your life matters, as do all other life forms. One small bird can bring beauty into your life. You can be a bird to many in the way you resonate your inner beauty, while playing your spiritual tune!

As Fragments ascend from Earth into the Fifth Plane of Evolution on the First Level, a great change occurs amid the Ascended Fragments on the higher levels above. Every experience on Earth has birthed new ways to exist. Those new ways were originally created by the Prime Force of The Oneness, directed by The Prime Fragment. With the influence of newly aspiring Spirit who return to The Upper Astral with acquired new ideas, those in the Third to Seventh Levels on The Fifth Plane of Evolution, will have to adapt to create new inventions that, in time, will be shared by Fragments that incarnate at a time suitable for change to occur. We are happy to inform you that, at this time, you are all ready for change. Though you may complain on your Planet about how bad things are, we say, we see separation, annihilation of what was and the birth of what is to come. We are excited for you to enjoy the arising of new input from The Oneness, where all have a common goal. Unity!

Unity is necessary at various stages of assimilation. What was, is, and will be, must be accepted in harmony with what is in The Oneness. On Earth, unity is considered to be an integration of ideals, hopes and dreams, none of which applies in The Oneness. Remember, all that is created within the Fifth Plane of Evolution is only a command to deconstruct or reconstruct life into a new order of existence on Earth, where the birthing of new ways to exist, feeds fuel to your fire and to The Oneness.

We exist to keep you safe. We are the keepers of time and of all forms. This was our assignment in the beginning of creation, and as such, it will always be so. Do we shift and change in consciousness? Yes, relative to the battles and ways of existence. The Oneness is flexible as are you in your coding. Ascension and Descension is just our mode of growth and spiritual activities. We are never without support and growth. You are our expressions in form. You are our experiences in form. You are one with us and all that is.

To make things clearer, we would like to explain how the Seven Levels of Earth, *(Forth Plane of Evolution)* are perceived by all incarnated humans in your world, as you pass from life to life. We will give examples throughout a Spirit's journey in existences of the Forth Plane of Evolution that you can relate to. We will also give an example of the mirror image of the other six Planes of Evolution, and their involvement in the existence of all that is. The 'I AM!'

CHAPTER ELEVEN
I am ALL That I Am!

In the last chapter we promised to lay before you a journey through the Levels of the Fourth Plane of Evolution. We will begin our story before the incarnation of our Fragment is made manifest. We will call our incarnate Fragment Aron and follow his journey as a Spirit Entity in embodiment, as well as his return to The Astral Levels of the Forth Plane of Evolution, Known as *The Lower & Upper Astral,* as our example. While we make it clear we cannot itemize all his lives, we can give a general overview of his Ascension, while integrating with those in Descension. You will see, by our examinations and explanations, how he and we have evolved together in various ways through Divine Love and Divine Wisdom, as he exchanges energy from life to life. In this way, his life generates friction that reverberates, causing resonation and, yes, rejuvenation, which allows us all to transform. Thus the Oneness continues in all its glory.

In the Upper Astral, friends gathered together. They were of one mind. An inner calling was pulling them together. A sense of need then gave birth to an awakening. A shift was about to occur in the force of The Oneness. Immediately, this group of Fragments began to assimilate one another's energies, taking on their memories, their Archetypes, and their whole Soul Codings that instantly combined. They had arrived at a glorious state of unity.

They immediately were assimilating and instinctively making choices. Each had defined their roles on Earth, and each was ready to be incarnated. Each Fragment then became a Spirit, who individually selected their own chosen Spiritual Soul Structure Coding, inborn from the Prime Fragment. They were collectively encoded within their roles to instigate a large productive change on Earth. Each Spirit was ready to establish free will within self on Earth. Their independent survival would unravel this large Soul Group, as each incarnated at designated moments of transformation. Individually, they had, and likely, will always have, spiritual ribbons of unity that tie them to families and important friends who will fuel their lives with emotional responses. Each will, in turn, share experiences emotionally. They each had a built-in network that always allows them to connect in Spirit or even in Human form, where planned. Yes, Aron was to be the Prime Fragment, incarnated as a Guru. His Spirit form would incarnate as a spiritual leader.

Then, one by one, each was born into families far from one another. How could Spirits that were meant to work, marry, or do something fun together, meet? On Earth, everyone has their own personal story. They each are born and given guardianship until old enough to make choices.

The Age of Independence is dormant until an awakening occurs, caused by a sudden happening. From this point on, we will give a simple outline of our Spirit Aron's journeys back and forth from Earth and the Astral Levels of Ascension and Descension.

The First Level:

Aron was feeling very afraid. He could hear the sounds of the great beast. He growl and howled. He would stand his ground. His mate came to his side, eyes pleading. He pushed her aside and stepped forward. He howled and yelled and screamed until he was dizzy. Then suddenly he was tossed high and floating until he met the sky. Aron wondered what had happened. Somehow he could now speak. Then he saw her. So beautiful and sweet. She seemed familiar. She came to him and put a hand on his shoulder. A shiver ran up his spine and suddenly he was laughing. He knew he was in The Oneness with Lucretia, his mentor. He had embraced his first lesson of *Pride* with a coding of *Stubbornness*. He had had no appreciation of love, only a desire to exist for as long as he could. He had led his people as far as he could too. All living things were dying as the atmosphere thickened with dust. His last stand against the Great Giant Beast was all that was left to do, while the others escaped.

Back in the Lower Astral, Lucretia visited him often as he assimilated this last life. She taught him how pride is considered by many to be evil or stupid. She taught him to understand more about his native instincts and the happenings he dealt with during that life. Again and again, she returned to him to teach him more about his existence and potential, until he asked to live on Earth again. When she felt he was finally ready to focus on his existence as a leader, she prepared him for another life. Their bond was eternal. This time he was encoded with a Goal of Rejection and Modes of Power, Caution, and Investigation. This lower personality part of his Soul Structure Coding was still evolving. Spirits incarnating from The Dark levels of the Third Plane of Evolution can only work with the lower coding of the Soul Structure. As a Fragment evolves in Ascension, so more of their spiritual coding is revealed.

Aron incarnated many times. His forms of action were often a surprise to him. Once he was a medicine man who called the Gods, Guardians of the Earth, who came and gave him great power. He danced in his delights and was one with his Gods. This life ended in disease where his magic could cure no one. Back in The Lower Astral, on the sixth Level, he awakened to love and so evolved to the Seventh Level of The Third Plane of Evolution.

Here on this new Level, Aron was beginning to understand that emotions have extremes in opposing physical sensations. After several educational experiences in upgrading his spiritual

106

understandings of his part in The Oneness, he prepared for a new life on Earth. Once again he joined with those who would unite with him. As before, many came in groups of thousands, some to be his friends and some his enemies.

Aron wanted to study himself in combat, and to be encoded with a Goal of Acceptance versus a Chief Feature of Self-destruction. He expected his life to be hard but was ready for the task! He had made his choice without Lucretia's input and she was there to support him yet again, while he was incarnated.

Once again, one by one, Spirits he had bonded with, incarnated. He found he had a new skill born out of his emotional bond with them all. He felt connected to them all and often saw and felt aspects of their lives as they lived, preparing the way for his return. When the Spirits returned to The Astral, to stand beside him once again, he saw that their plan was well conceived, and that each incarnated Spirit in physical action was causing shifts in earthly ways. There were often times of joy, sadness, loss, and the list of emotions goes on. On Earth, Aron's job was to be a war hero, a leader of men! He was a part of a big event, to create a united world!

Aron was born into a typical low cast Roman Family. He had grown up with an elder brother, whom he admired and loved deeply. Galilee was where his father had been stationed before being sent across the sea, never to return. On one hot day, the Roman Army came to their village. They had orders to enlist the eldest sons of each family to become a soldier for overseas wars. Each family in the village lost a son that day. Aron had high hopes that his brother would return. The years passed, as he practiced with his father's sword, a keepsake his mother had given him on his twelfth birthday. He had never known his father, who had been killed in some war far away, and whom he never could forget. There was something in the way his mother talked about his father and her love for him. She kept his memory as a figure head of his family. What he did in those early years, was to honor and pray for his return, which kept him alive in Aron's mind. He used to tell himself that he would come home sometime.

When, his brother was about to be taken from him, he felt enraged! At that time, he was young and thoughtless, pleading for his brother to be allowed to stay to help his mother, while offering to go in his brother's place. The result of this confrontation and fighting talk, led to them both being taken into the army.

Aron learned quickly and following several years of proven valor while fighting the enemy, was made a Legionnaire; a more noble form of office. He had long lost contact with his brother and had never been home since he had been taken and trained to kill. There was a hunger in him. A desire for company. He lusted after women and drank himself almost to death, when one night he had a dream. In that dream, his Guardian Angel Lucretia spoke to him. She told him to accept his lessons in using anger, rage, loss, isolation, and emotional hatred. He then cried in her lap. She whispered in his ear. "You are their leader. Rise up and rebel! Use your rage for good."

Of course he awoke with a start! He was visibly shaken. All that day he tried to forget this vivid dream. It made no sense to him. His men followed his command and there was no issue to fight for. In fact, they were on sabbatical leave. Over the following weeks, that turned into months, the men grew angry. There was no food, supplies were cut off and men were starting to arise in anger. Aron fought off his ideas, while the memory of his dream arose time and time again. In time, he was in agreement with his men, and so he led his men to begin a revolution. Yes, many died, but their uprising caused a shift in the people they left behind. Soon other countries revolted and finally Rome fell! All this happened because Aron followed his coding. We in The Oneness were full of joy. The Shift of a new Age had begun. All Ascended Fragments were busy assimilating all that had happened. Those who returned to us from Earth were well received.

Much later, Aron was then a Fragment living in the Upper Astral, who was still a Spirit in form. He was able to do whatever he had a desire to do. His main focus was to evolve, and so he sought out more Ascended Fragments to sit with, and learn from them, as they talked about The Oneness and its promises. Incidentally, promises are always made in The Astral, where they become encoded into the Spirit-self. All promises made between the Ascended Fragments, and those who are of the Dark Third Plane of Evolution, are made long before the next incarnation of a Spirit is to occur. Each connection is then encoded into the chosen Soul Structure Coding, which in turn is transferred into the heart of the Fetus in the womb, where it is actively absorbing the mother-to-be's complete emotional and mental experiences that have occurred throughout her life.

This emotional bond is spiritual in nature. Its purpose is to define the personality and character of the child-to-be, as their Spirits bond together within mother's Heart Chakra. This is called a Spirit Ribbon or cord. It should be stated here that since the dawn of your time, this has been the way for incarnating Spirits to bond with mothers. Those early incarnations were without understanding. Their animalistic traits focused on existence, experiences in survival and a growing belief in some great Spirit who watches over them. These early Fragments who incarnated as Spirits into Human form were watched very closely. Indeed all animals were observed and stimulated according to Soul Structure Codings that instilled a desire to feel and belong to one another on Earth.

Aron had decided he had had enough male lives and wanted to be born as a girl this time. It was his first emotional step towards Divine Love. We will call Aron, Aronia.

Aronia was born to a wealthy family in India. Her family assured her she had a long history of renowned ancestors, and that it was important she follow in their footsteps. Throughout her life she did as she was told. Often she felt ashamed that she was so beautiful. Other girls made her life misery. She found it hard to make friends. In time, she married the man her father chose for her. He was a gentle elderly man who only visited her bed now and then. She gave him a son and later a daughter. She lived a simple but happy life until her husband died from a sudden heart attack.

She sobbed for days, mourning the loss of her husband. She prayed for his soul to make the journey into the arms of Vishnu. Then she prayed for herself. She had no means of support. She needed help! Her doubt in the power of Vishnu was weak. She felt she did not deserve help. God had made her beautiful and that was all she knew about herself. She had no choice but to return home. When she arrived, she was dismayed to find that an outbreak of a water disease had killed everyone except her youngest sister who was still a child. Now a widow with three children to feed, she was lost. That night she cried like a baby. She had no idea what to do, or how to provide for them all. It was cold and the night was long. She tossed and turned praying for an answer from God, but He was silent.

The next morning was sunny. The cool day was beginning to heat up. She stood outside at the tap, waiting her turn to get some fresh water, when a man came up to her. He looked her up and down and then asked her, "Do you speak their language?"
She wondered what he meant. Her eyes asked the question while she remained silent.

"I have need of someone who can read and write, can you?" He asked.

She nodded and he invited her to bring her family to his house.

What followed was a life's work of loyalty to this man, who had taken her in at a time when all seemed lost. She truly believed he had been sent by God that morning. She learned over the years to love, honor, and respect him and his work, which involved teaching the young ones to read and write. Little had she ever imagined her lessons in hand communication on paper would become one of the most important forms of communication in what was to be the future of India. Her lessons she taught, were usually in groups outside huts where they lived. Her work was vital to the ebb and flow of The Oneness. Because of her intense work ethics, the children she taught had someone to give them counsel and guidance. She was in their eyes, a true teacher who loved them dearly. She died peacefully in her sleep with a joyous reunion with her husband who had been observing the greatness of her work.

Aronia was once again reunited with all her loved ones, who had gone before her to pave the way for her life as a woman. Upon arriving back in the Astral, her heart was open to embrace the essence of Divine Love and Wisdom. Birthing children as a woman for the first time had opened up her soul to the acceptance of spiritual growth and her own desire to ascend into The Oneness.

Many other lives were to follow, each lived in the forms of both male and female in a variety of countries. As each life was completed and assimilated, Aron grew more and more towards embracing the light of the Fifth Plane of Evolution. He instinctively knew that it was time to incarnate into the Forth Level on Earth once again. But this time, for a different purpose.

That of embracing Divine Wisdom, which would eventually be entwined with Divine Love within his physical life.

Since we really know you can identify with Aron's journey until now, we will fast forward through many of his/her lives as he/she incarnated time and time again. In each life lived, there was always a calling to express love in its various form. We could tell his/her stories of murder and subterfuge, but we prefer to tell stories of lessons and the evolvements that are turning points in a Fragments ascension into the next level. Throughout Aron's entire journeys on Earth, he had ascended and had acquired millions of spiritual bonds. He had, by then, become a knowing part of The Oneness.

Our story continues in the desert lands of Earth. Here Arabs dwelled, living around an Oasis, making a living in trading goods. Camels were the norm, and life was generally quiet until the tribes rebelled. Into this much changed world, Aron incarnated to follow the lessons of his father, who cherished him more than his elder sisters. As he grew up, he learned the ways of the desert, the songs of praise for life, and the joy of watching his family entertain one another with stories of ancient tales. Aron was hooked by his lifestyle. At an early age he watched his camel being born. Something inside him stirred as this amazing animal arrived into life! It was as though he was experiencing his own birth from his mother's womb. Aron felt himself bonding with this animal as she entered his world, and whom he was then told, was his responsibility to rear, feed and love always, for she would take him far across the desert to a new land.

The years passed as he grew, married, and had children, who also grew up and made him a grandfather. Life had been a happy one until one day an army of strangers arrived. His harem of camels had evolved from his faithful first camel, who sadly died, but whose seed was in her young ones, who Aron also loved.

Trade had been good over the years, and his camels faithful to the routes they took across the desert, where trade was fair in major cities around the desert. Now into his world came men with weapons that he had never seen. Whenever he had made the journey to trade, he always made it a ritual. The night sky was his guide, a message from The Oneness to trust his instincts and wisdom. On this last trip he had felt uneasy earlier that night. His life ended abruptly. Moment before his own death, the sound of an explosion shocked him as he watched his son die. Instantly, an awakened deep-seeded memory flared up within him. He knew the prophesied war had just begun and there was no stopping it. He new their deaths would lead to war!

A revolution had reached his land and he and his sons were the first examples of unnatural death. His life of peace had come to an end, but not before he had taught his children to protect themselves from strangers. His encoded Soul Structure Coding had all that he needed to guide his family. His younger sons, when they heard of his death and of their elder two brothers, rose up to begin the revolution that was to last for years between the twelve tribes. Never again was unity to be found. This was key to the ascension of all Fragments who incarnate. Wars became the norm! A new Age was begun.

Aron stayed in the Spirit World, moving between the Dark Levels of the Third Plane of Evolution. He focused on assisting Fragments to incarnate on Earth in various places defined as Levels one to five, mentioned in this book. Helping newly evolved Dark Fragments to incarnate and then to interact with the darkness of war was hard for him. Their ruthlessness was necessary, as they evolved through various situations where cruelty and destruction was the norm. Evolution was consistently occurring as The Oneness re-assessed and evolved allowing many new fragments from The Dark Side of life to incarnate on Earth. Thus it was that the dark and light entwined and still is actively doing so. This awakening of lesser evolved Fragments, now incarnating with negative activities has brought The Oneness into its own test. It questions its own evolution. What followed was philosophy, religious order, counseling, and reformation over eons of time. Each Fragment was awakened with instinct to embrace the paranormal aspects of The Oneness. The battle on Earth was established. Then and now, the Light of Love Divine is tested versus the Darkness of Wisdom.

Over many periods of your history, Descending Spirits from the Fifth Plane of Evolution have incarnated on Earth too. Their task has always been to teach about the beauty of creation on all Levels of both Ascension and Descension. Any interaction of any Fragment, whether in Human or Spirit form, or simply purely using temporary forms that allows an Ascended Master to communicate, will be integrated and enhanced, within the Soul Structure Coding as the Fragment enters life.

Many Ancient Souls are incarnated into your world in order to keep the existence of unity, balance, and harmony when any destructive incidents occur. Each negative occurrence involves both the individuals who are only focused on their immediate existence, to also include those who are born aware and ready to take the lead, when the time comes. To this end, Aron aspired and succeeded in assisting many Fragments to incarnate and ascend in vibration, to embrace The Oneness as he himself had done so long ago.

Ancient Masters can manifest in any form that has existed in The Oneness. This is possible since every Spirit that has been incarnated into form is available for them to choose. They can even appear as animals! As these great sages can incarnate at any time in earthly Eras, they have been able to influence Spirits in human forms to walk their correct pathways. Everyone's pathway leads to a drama, where questions about purpose and fate arise. Instinctively, any Human will search for enlightenment. There is always an awakening, when a lost or lower Spirit is calling for assistance and support. Immediately help is given, whether it is to die for a revolutionary cause or from a natural death.

Let us speak of accidents that occur unexpectedly. A Spirit in human form could become careless and, as a result, end a life suddenly. If this should occur, a great wave of grief floods the Earth. Such an event would be an example of a beloved Queen dying, or land being conquered where many are killed in a battle. In your time, many die from accidents caused from bombs and mines. Too many suffer now, but their suffering will awaken future incarnated Spirits to prevent this from happening again. Wars are a thing of the past now. It is time for peace, unity and sharing. This will not come easily to Humans who will still argue about ways and mean to find peace. In this way, when passion emerges, peace will rise and fall once again. Any conflict will cause a new flow of energy, not only around your world, but in all of The Oneness too!

This spiritual energy will not only be felt in your world, but in all other worlds in existence. Your life, and those you incarnated with are collectively the corner stone of change. What happens on Earth, happens elsewhere, though you may never know it consciously, while inwardly, your instincts will let you know that your Universe is changing as are all other Universes within The Oneness.

Aron is now an Ascended Master who has reached the Second Level of the Fifth Plane of Evolution. Here he can select other Fragments in Descension to work with him to establish peace on Earth. They use counter-messages to create confusion. Conflict ensues creating stimulus for those who are incarnated, as the billions of Humans, who are born to ensure that changes will occur. Your world, at this point of your evolution, is of great importance to The Cosmos. Energy from your planet vibrates within its own Universe. The sounds it resonates are the collective actions of Humans, animals, other creatures in form, that together oscillate with that of Earth natural core. Earth, in turn, vibrates other Universes and so on, until all are aware that some 'thing' unnamed or unknowable is being stimulated, causing a rift in The Cosmic Energy of all that is in form. This is then seen as the battle between The Dark and Light Sides of all existences.

In this great awakening there is a Cosmic Pause. This very special *spiritual pause* is a moment of *supreme enlightenment* when all Fragments on all Levels are reconnected to The Prime Fragment, that stimulates balance through its unique moment of sharing. This new vibration and resonation is a healing energy which oscillates within each Fragment, creating harmony and balance, uniting all Fragments. A yearning for peace arises in all dimensions of existence. There is no sound! Only silence and peace without judgment. Divine Wisdom and Divine Love are entwined in utter bliss as they generate unity in stillness. Then a physical shock wave is released throughout The Cosmos. All Planes of Evolution and all Levels in each Plane immediately respond, forming new structures to provide stability to the ebb and flow of The Oneness. A new beginning is upon all.

When unity is established, action begins. New energy surges as, once again, Fragments continue to live and die on Earth and then to evolve further through the Levels of The Fifth Plane of Evolution. Aron no longer assists Spirits existing within the Third Plane of Evolution but does connect with Humans on the Fourth Plane of Evolution on Earth. Occasionally he appears to incarnated Spirits he is watching over, while awakening them to a new inspirational understanding, in realizing their next step along their pathway.

He can appear as male or female, animal, or flower. He can speak around a person without form; enter the body of a Human and move them to save their life or teach them in meditation. He can do this with thousands of individuals on any Level of Ascension. He leads them towards The Light, imbued along by with his own Ascension into the light, that is pure vibrational sound on the Sixth Plane of Evolution.

On the Sixth Plane of Evolution, visual and audio records of all forms captured from the lives of all Fragments are stored as memories, spoken words in all languages, along with the vibrations of all moods, and so much more that you cannot understand. Remember, sound and physical forms carry a tune! Aron's work in The Oneness is ongoing and extremely vital. All information is available to all, once each understand how the transformation of sounds, far beyond your physical senses, carry information to be downloaded according to need.

All evolving Fragments ascending through the Seven Levels on The Fifth Plane of Evolution, are each resonating an extremely refined vibration. For most, there is little known or understood when their personal transformation occurs, especially in the lower Levels and Planes of Evolution. When such an occasion occurs, a Fragment in the Lower Planes of Evolution is usually mystified by sensations of physical feelings. Then connections instantly happen with an Ascended Master Soul Group that is currently incarnated with a purpose. That experience will then be an informative awakening of what needs to be done, to bring about change between the Lower, Upper Astral and in the existence of life on Earth.

The more refined Levels of the Fifth Plane of Evolutions provide spiritual support and strong connections with The Sixth Plane of Evolution. On the Third through Seventh Levels of this Fifth Plane of Evolution, Spirit Fragments begin to amalgamate their experiences from both their Dark and Light incarnations, which when completed are shared throughout all Levels in all

Planes of Evolution. Assimilation and balance are of supreme importance as they collectively transform their energies, in uniting and creating new forms as befitting all transformational occurrences, that arise on Earth and elsewhere in your Universe.

Their spiritual transformation can be understood through the study of musical notes. The Major key of C has, within it, all flat and sharp notes entwined. If you could play all notes together you would have a sound that would be within your hearing range, but unbearable to listen to. Your thoughts would snap, and your emotions become unbalanced. Now let us put this idea into much lower or higher scales where notes are beyond Human range. You would not hear it, but instead would feel it. By attuning to what your body feels, you will speculate, and in one tiny part of your being, accept a minute part of the message being sent to you along with an overall feeling that something is about to happen.

Your message might be a feeling to go home immediately. When you arrive home, you find a friend who is frantically trying to get help to save their house from burning down, while you too have to protect your own home. Others may have instant sensations that leave a knowing message. A scary thought of an airplane crashing and your fear for your family dying in it, can later be understood, when you find out that a plane, has indeed crashed, with no one you know having anything to do with the crash! Then, without knowing why, you cry. The reason could well be that one of your Soul Mate Fragments has just died in that plane accident.

We could give you many examples of how the Sixth Plane of Evolution works to keep harmony and balance on Earth. We must give you credit to know that through your emotional and mental psyche, you feel what happens to other members of your Soul Group, who are incarnated at the same time as you, and live somewhere else far away. The purpose of separation on Earth is mirror-imaged in the Sixth Plane of Evolution. These great wise integrated Fragments are the back bone of The Oneness. Every Fragment on all Levels is busy constantly attuning and retuning the vibrations of not only all Fragments incarnated, but all births in the Dark Side of new forms and their beginnings. They also support and assist in the transformation of all, as they evolve toward integrating with The Prime Fragment, and on into an understanding of their own unified ascension as a Universal Soul. Perhaps you may call them angels, since they often enter your dreams, and your meditations.

When a Fragment enters the Seventh Level of the Sixth Plane of Evolution, having passed up through the Seven Levels of Ascension, they have been assimilated and will either separate and begin to Descend towards embodiment on Earth again, or be absorbed into the Prime Fragment. On This Seventh Plane of Evolution there are only three physically aware levels. The other four levels are where the combined experiences and lessons of Ascended Soul Groups are released and shared with The Primal Fragment, some drizzling down to the Lower Planes of Evolution.

What has gone before physically is assimilated as one big awakening on the First Level of the Seventh Plane of Evolution. Here, all Fragments now integrated, begin combining all aspects of knowing, to become one seemingly United Fragment embracing Divine Wisdom. The First Level is where each Fragment's spiritual journey is integrated with that of other Fragments in their Soul Group. Their collective thoughts amalgamate in becoming all knowing. Each Fragment, as part of this Ascended Soul Group, will assimilate one another until they are all fully integrated, becoming one evolved group who understand all that is! What follows is a desire to mutually become the Light of Earth!

All absorbed Soul Groups are engrossed in absorbing and working with Divine Wisdom that is imparted to Lower incarnating Fragments as well as sharing with The Primal Fragment. In this way, new insights challenge wisdom from long ago, when recorded past experiences, now recovered as Universal Modes, awakens various states of awareness for change. This newly made awareness of Divine Wisdom is then shared back down into the Sixth and Fifth Planes of Evolution, ensuring that the battle continues within the Forth Plane of Evolution, where Fragments are receptive to new ideas, ways and means of living, while also knowing instinctively that they are supported by The Oneness.

When a Universal Soul amalgamates with other Universal Souls on the second Level of the Seventh Plane of Evolution, Divine Love manifests in an exceptionally wonderful show of sharing emotional bonds with all Fragments, on all Levels, in all Planes of Evolution. Here both Divine Wisdom and Love must find harmony and inner peace. Once unity of Ascended Soul Groups are united, they begin their existence on the Third Level. This last physical Level of Human/Spiritual consciousness with their experiences are entwined with other species from other parts of The Cosmos. Parallels of understanding arise as unification is accepted. All past forms from any aspect of life is united in one loving symbolic hug. Fragments on the Forth to Seventh Levels are assimilated into The Oneness, becoming a part of The Prime Fragment, where the bond of Divine Love unifies the changes that will later motivate actions, with new forms then created. Together they exist as interactive energy that constantly creates friction and expansion of The Prime Soul Fragments.

These last four Levels of Ascension are also the overlapping Planes of a Fragment's descending journey. Now encoded with a new beginning for The Oneness, These Soul Groups begin to break away as they descend through the 1st to 4th Levels. Here a merger happens instinctively. Energy rebounds within itself, causing great waves of energy to build up. That energy tightens until it creates friction. Then, with a great need for release, shifts and separates sending energy back down through all Levels, on all Planes of Existence. New forms are created, and a new story begins. Once again The Prime Fragment is changed and with its changes comes all changes below on every level.

So, what of us, your Seven Archangels, Masters of Creation in both the Dark and Light, you may ask? We are as you say cast "Outside the Box." We were given the power to create all forms and will continue to do so. Our support is what you call The Brotherhood, Holy Ghost/Spirit and much more. We are your parents, your guardians, and collectively, your savior for all Fragments on all levels of existence. Your lives are our lives. Every Fragment's journey is our journey. For this reason, you can understand that it was our energy that gave you life and will continue to do so. We are not above or below any forms. We exist for you to exist. We all exist for The Oneness to continue in an ever-evolving vibration of unity, as one very large family that knows how to integrate our various ways and means of existences, which compliments and sometimes stirs up the balance of unity to cause dilemmas with puzzles to be solved.

In ending this journey into the light, be often reminded that you are equal, and in many ways, different from others, without competition or judgment. To make your life have meaning, listen to us, listen to your brothers and sisters, and all others. The Change is coming, and you have an important role to play! You are all our voices. You are all our thoughts from all aspects of all things ever created. You have a million and one choices to make, and you will make them with freedom of choice, no matter the circumstances. Always stop and ask yourself, what led me to this point in my life, and then ask yourself, how much do you appreciate your journey and all your interactions with so many friends and enemies? Once you have found unity in your personal soul search, you will find us ready to teach you more. So be it! Embrace that part of you that is the "I AM" of The Oneness.

THE FINAL CHAPTER
In The End Is The Beginning And In The Beginning Is Choice!

In the beginning we explained our purpose in writing this book, so that you may individually understand why you reincarnate, time and time again. Here we wish you to know that there are stories within stories. Everyone has a story that seems to end with a following beginning that offers choice. Your world has over seven billion Humans who are all processing their lives by remembering their different personal stories, over and over again. Meanwhile when they join up for a cause, there is now a bigger story with many greater stories to entwine themselves in. Once, there was a time, when that was enough to keep the ebb and flow of The Oneness in harmony.

In your era of time, there is much more to consider now. Through the birth of the Technical Age ,you are now able to know people in foreign parts. You can chat with them online and trade to make financial gains. Others live in poverty, depending on their phones to keep them connected with the rest of the world. So, as you say, "It is now a small world," upon which you live. Each of you has your Spirit living inside your body that is yearning to be listened to. Your brains are on over-drive and are breaking down. Diseases and maladies create illnesses and death.

Those Humans who are passing back into The Oneness, returning to the Seventh Level of the Third Plane of Evolution will aspire to ascend into the Upper Astral. Their future will be motivated to integrate themselves with the Upper Astral on the First Level of The Fifth Plane of Evolution. Meanwhile those Fragments in Descension will incarnate with Soul Structure Codings that both protects them from their wrong choices and ensures they complete their mission. That mission will be to aid in rebuilding your world.

The First Level of The Upper Astral is liken to Heaven. Here Spirits congregate and assist one another to make plans of action for when they incarnate again. The Upper Astral and Lower Astral Levels combine to give Earth, The Forth Plane of Evolution, four spiritual Levels that you will reincarnate from. Each Level is liken in many ways to the Seven Earthly physical Levels in all other Planes of Evolution.

When we speak of each Spirit reincarnating on each of the Earth Levels over and over again, we must also state here that you also return to its equal level in The Astral. There you process the last life lived, with all other lives you have lived, while assimilating them to awaken further plans for evolvement. Then you will choose another Level in the Astral to reincarnate from. Variety is the spice of life! Life continually changes on your planet and so there are plenty of opportunities for lots of experiences to be tasted, smelled, seen, heard, done, and observed. All it takes to awaken, is to know that all emotional responses to stimuli and The Earth will always provide you with plenty to keep you occupied.

Reminding you that Descending Fragment are also passing by through many of these Astral Levels, allowing for an integration and harmony within a single opposing pair, couples, or large groups. As these Ascended Ones integrate with the Descending Ones there are lessons passed on to one another. Also, another thing of great importance which you might call the "The hub," is where the dark and light harmonizes in all Fragments now in Spirit form.

For a short moment they accept one another as part of all that is. They become neutral, locked in a Divine Pause, resting from the long battle of survival. They exist without purpose. At that same moment, there is an inner sense of being still, silent and at peace. This is akin to taking a deep breath and then exhaling. Nothing matters but existence. This amazing moment is a direct reflection of peace, stillness and silence sent from The Prime Fragment. Spirits experiencing this inner most peaceful moment are reprogrammed, stimulated to listen, and learn as they are prepared for things to come.

The Astral becomes a very busy place with lots of learning in understanding and embracing the story of evolution with Divine Wisdom and Love. As Fragments evolve from the Third Plane of Evolution with a desire to ascend, they incarnate on Earth to live lives in a variety of fundamental ways, experiencing hardships, while learning to improvise, invent and explore their surroundings in the more remote places on your Planet, such as The Poles, Swamps and Jungles, where survival is truly tested. Those from the Upper Astral will incarnate in the Plains and Cities around the world to instigate growth in spiritual awareness, such as religious and alternative ways of connecting with their Ascended Soul Groups, in order to bring new inventions and beliefs into form!

Many Young and Older Souls are incarnating into your world now. They will become leaders and students who have descended into form for the purpose of congregating, to establish order out of chaos and love out of pain. Rejoice! The Great Aquarian Age is upon you. Reach out to embrace cosmic consciousness now, since you are all in preparation for a great transformation. Energy is expressed in all forms. A new culture will arise and with it further emotional contact with understanding and purpose. You are all our precious children of your Universe and beyond. Awaken and embrace your true identity and become the person you want to be, born from out of your coding and inheritance, with free will to become a known part of The Oneness on Earth.

IN CONCLUSION BY DR. MARGARET
The Overlap of The Great Piscean & Aquarian Ages

Understanding the overlap of the Piscean Age with the Aquarian Age can be mind-boggling when we look back over the last few centuries. The ending of The Great Piscean Age began with a general awakening to useless suffering of the Peoples of Earth, during the late 1800's. Individuals began to face their insecurities, giving rise to possessiveness along with culture differences that seemed to be an impossible problem to solve.

Though I could mention many incidents that arose over two hundred years ago, it is important here to say that under the overlap of The Great Aquarian Age, women began to find their voice and to work towards their emancipation, and equality with men. The feminine aspect is within all of us, however, the Great Piscean Age had, for thousands of years, controlled the feminine aspects of life, by enslaving women's roles, relative to the needs of a controlling male society. Men were adamant that women were second class citizens, who needed to be controlled, since they were considered incapable of learning economics, or in administering estates, or developing businesses run by men who provided the material things needed in life.

Meanwhile women, being mothers and homebuilders, were expected to do as their masters, husband, and other males in their family bid, doing all without question. Should they disobey, they were often locked away in asylums for life. In other countries, such as The Far East, women were killed for disobeying men over very simple issues. A woman generally had no value beyond birthing a new generation to continue the family line.

So much suffering on the part of women led eventually to various uprisings in The West. Women Like Florence Nightingale, The Suffragettes, and others, too many to mention here, evolved in independence throughout the 19th & 20th Centuries. Women who stood for new laws, the right to vote and much later, to then become politicians and owners of their own companies, took us all into The Great Aquarian Age. Their independence from men has taken over two hundred years and is still ongoing in many parts of the world.

However, all was not lost for men! Various Ascended Masters incarnated amongst them. Carl Jung, born July 26th, 1875 was such a man, who through his own spiritual awareness, embraced the paranormal and metaphysical approaches to new points of view about himself. His evolved teachings were considered revolutionary by the turn of the century. Under the protection of Sigmund Freud, psychology inspired even more followers who were of like mind to change one's point of view about life in general. Men argued and fought over both political and family issues, while women developed tact, learned to listen well, and studied privately to ensure a better future for herself, should her man fail to take care of her. Women in pioneer countries often had to take the lead in running their family's business affairs while her husband was far away on business ventures. When he returned, she calmly would step down and attend to household duties.

In later times. Following the aftermath of WWI & WWII, when so many died needlessly, an awakening from The Oneness was generally released to all those Fragments living on Earth. That awakening was the introduction of The Great Aquarian Age of Enlightenment and Evolution, yet to come. Individuals began to talk about the 1000 years of peace to come. Women begun to do the work of men! They often battled just to have a foot-standing position in some way that would lead for other women to follow. Without Florence Nightingale and the Crimea war, I would never have been able to study medicine after WWII ended.

Today, as a result of those who have gone before, we have become extremely aware of our wrong-doings. The long lists of harm done would go, on and on, when we think about a woman's journey from slavery to freedom, in any land you care to mention, and over any time period from Ages past too! The Great Piscean Age was about being in command, by conquering, owning, and controlling situations, as was said earlier in this book, founded on The Chief Feature of Greed. As the years passed, individuals were becoming aware that the value of life was important. So much suffering, brought about by the many wars that had occurred throughout this Great Piscean Age, eventually led to the feminine arising and the emancipation of women.

I would like you to visualize two circles overlapping one another creating an elliptical oval between them. The Great Piscean Age was embedded within the new Great Aquarian Age long before it begun. Its influential overlap was to awaken individuals to freedom and choice. Meanwhile the elliptical oval of The Great Aquarian Age was already entwined with The Great Piscean Age in astrological dynamic aspect of the last two centuries, as it drew to a close. These two Great Ages have been overlapped effectively for quite some time. If we go back to the late nineteenth century, we see the beginnings of the closure of the ways and means of survival throughout this Great Piscean Age.

Bearing in mind, that you now know there exists friction in all The Planes of Evolution within The Oneness, and that friction is vital to its existence, making it possible for all Fragments to ascend and descend consistently, you can now see how The Archangels, like us who are incarnated on Earth, have also been through their ups and downs relative to our earthly activities in evolution. That is not to say that they have or will solve all our problems, but rather to say that we have come to a point of awareness where we understand that illusion is history, and that history does not need to be repeated.

Some may argue that illusion can lead to fantasy and eventually to creation, and they would be right. It matters not whether the thing created is negative or positive. What does matter is that we learn from our mistakes. In 2008 we began to truly merge into The Great Aquarian Age. However, we have dragged our Piscean Age consciousness with us, in our acts of embracing change. In observation of the past twenty years, we see issues about races, politics, structure, languages and so many issues around how to integrate new rules and regulations that will suit everyone. The problem is that no two people think or feel alike! Yes, freedom does bring independency to choose. Choice to be alone is for contemplation, not for isolation or victimization. Choice gives everyone an opportunity to speak and share, as well as to listen well.

Now that we are fully supported and embraced by The Great Age of Aquarius, we are beginning to understand that we each have homework to do on ourselves. If we cannot find harmony within the way we think and feel, and subsequently act in peace, then we will be doomed for further wars. It should be clearly understood here that The Oneness will not interfere in the way we make our changes as a world nation of Humans. We can take as long as we like to understand that peace comes from listening, understanding, adapting, and uniting with plans that may change, but which will begin a new revolution in Mankind's point of view in how we integrate our species. At this time of writing we see peace marches as well as violence in many countries all over our Planet. We as a united Human race are in a destructive mode. Generally speaking, we all want the old ways gone and the new ways integrated for the betterment of Mankind. Problem is no one wants to let anything go for fear of loss.

Unfortunately, today the influences of Pisces is still with us. Greed and loss go hand in glove! There are many countries suffering with wars, local uprisings, drought, floods, starvation, The Corona Virus, impractical leads, and the list goes on. We are in a birthing stage of becoming acquainted with Mother Earth, in new ways never thought of by Humans. Indoor Pod farming will become more popular since local companies can supply people who live in their town, rather than relying on imports. Communications with technology are only just now beginning to make sense. As technological education increases for the average person, it will make it possible for new inventions with sound to be created.

Sound is key to the vibration of our future here on Earth. Earth has its own musical key notes, while each individual creates their own tune too. We have long discovered that music speaks to the Soul and not to the mind. When you listen to your favorite music, it heals you by unlocking blocks in your Etheric Body, allowing your physical body to heal. The Oneness is all about musical notes as we were told earlier by Archangel Haniel. When we are in harmony, our musical key note is always accessible and we feel happy. If we lose ourselves in self-pity, judgment, and depression, then we are in a state of generating musical sharp or flat notes that create discord, especially if both notes are entwining. Discords bring disruptions and decay.

As an observer of people, I have noticed a great deal of change in the influence of metaphysical studies. When I was only twenty-one, I was a rarity, in that, I was one of the few who could talk to Spirits, lost in The Dark or ascended in The Light, as though I am speaking to a person on Earth, the difference being I heard their voices within my head. I was then, and am now, telepathic with Spirits in The Oneness. People thought it was a gift. Now today, more and more children are being born today who are just like I was. They can pass on psychic messages in simple ways, see people making mistakes and question their surroundings. These very young ones are Old or Ascended Souls who have incarnated in Descension to learn materially about our world and to leave us with 'The Change' that will finally concluded in the next hundred and fifty or more years.

According to the Seven Archangels, each will influence Mankind once again as they have in Great Ages past. Their presence in our hearts and minds will become the accepted way of being a part of The Oneness. Psychology and Psychiatry will embrace an understanding of The Soul Structure Codings of each individual, but also of nations. Now that you know about the Forth Plane of Evolution here on Earth and your return to The Lower and Upper Astral, you can see how important it is for us all to integrate our species, accept philosophy and religions as simply an individual's way of connecting to The Oneness. Great spiritual gatherings will continue to arise, while other forms of artistic ways and means will evolve where unity abounds.

I realize that for many, this book will either be a revelation or be tossed aside by those not ready to let the old ways die. Yes, struggles will continue over the next 150 plus years, but as we draw closer to that time, we will have evolved a great deal. Here it is important to understand the influence of the Gemini energy as it manifest through the next two hundred years.

Gemini is known as The Twins, one wanting to go in one direction, while the other the opposite. For over 200 years or more we will find arguments, disagreements and yes, more skirmishes, but hopefully fewer wars. With a major transformation in the worlds weather patterns, we will adapt and recover from a variety of floods, earthquakes, and human disasters. You are already witnesses to this beginning, since it began occurring in 2013, when we first felt the influences of the dawn of the beginning of The Great Aquarian Age. We have seen violence in many forms, destruction caused by weather and Earth's plates shifting in the oceans of the world. More is yet to come!

We have also seen a great change in communications world-wide with what might be called talks, but which actually has educated us all, to know more about what is happening world-wide, especially since the Corona virus has caused us all to stay protected at home. Yes, its arrival was on time!

The Corona Virus is ancient and has awakened as our Poles melted. It is genetically able to transform itself relative to its environment. In the mirror-image of this single cell, we each must learn to adapt to survive once again. The young ones will embrace new ways of existence, while the older ones will pass back into The Oneness. By that time, this Earth will have much better ways of producing all that we need to survive, not in pain and anguish, but in harmony and peace.

To wind up here, an example for change in how we can heat our homes with solar panels shown to us already. The sun provides us with the warmth and the nurturing of Earth's needs, providing us too, with all that we need to be able to live here on Planet Earth. With the invention of solar panels to heat houses, and in myself, knowing that an ability to generate a new source of heat from reverberating sound that will keep a whole city warm, is on its way. I know we have stepped away from fossil fuels for warmth. The Piscean Age still lingers with needs for mining fuels and other precious gems etc. that people prize so much. Here we see the Chief Feature of Greed still clinging to the old ways. Archangel Haniel and Phaniel whose job will be to lead the following period beginning around 2250 AD, in our future. By then Phaniel will lead us towards unification of one species, Humans, who respect one another and work in harmony to ensure everyone's survival.

It is time to lift our heads out of the sands of time and awaken to the new ways our Earth can provide for us. In the times of Ancient Aliens, Babylonian people and even in The Great Ages of the past too, we have been left small clues to our bio-technically engineered bodies. We are now on the edge of understanding more about the amazing bio-chemistry of our existence. History maybe hidden from us under the earth, but the truth lies within each person's DNA. Every individual caries the story in their DNA and it is only a matter of time before more is understood about our evolvements here on Earth.

Whether you have had alien encounters, spoken to an alien guide, or simply like space novels and films, then you are already accessing some part of your DNA, where encoded within you is a history of the bio-engineering done so long ago. Here we are now, developing this same technology again. Where did it come from, this knowing how to do it in the first place? Well, those few old Descending Souls have incarnated bringing encoded instinctive DNA memories forward, while being stimulated to investigate and awaken to long lost knowledge. As they live their lives, their innate need to explore and create will manifest what they came to share with us.

With each challenge that arises, we struggle to find answers, and in some way, thanks to just one person or a group, new knowledge is found and shared. We are The Human Race, driven to find our beginnings in the past, while always seeking something new in our future. This driving force is apparent in each one of us. If we do not contribute to the world's ascension, then we would all be doomed to failure. Since no one wants to fail, we journey on, ever-looking for answers to our questions; why, how, when, what, who, where? If we could all manifest the answers to our questions, then we would indeed be absorbed into

The Oneness and Ascend into the arms of The Primal Fragment, called God.

My final advice, while hoping you enjoyed reading this book, is to encourage you to embrace change, taking great leaps with hopes and personal pride that abounds within you, to support yourself in being successful. Always know that each incarnated Spirit who make physical contact with you, is actually keeping a spiritual promise to connect in order to be a part of your life for a reason. Observe and learn from them. Give and share when you know they need you. Move on from what bores you or take a second look, since you may have been lazy.

This new century is all about change, and if you do not adapt, then you will be left behind, feeling miserable an unappreciated. However, if the worst comes to the worst, and you become enraged or miserable, at least you are contributing to the energy of The Oneness, so no life is ever a waste of time. Be a joyful part and contribute, in as many ways as you can, to discover just how generous we can all be together to create a new harmonious world to live on, as we Humans evolve in Oneness.

I have seen the future far ahead. Inter-marriages, inter-relationships, inter-breeding with so many new ways of building homes and doing business at our fingertips. New bio-technical engineering ways beyond our technical abilities now will develop new ways of regenerating tissue. Humanity will arise in a new form.

For now, always Remember that your life has purpose! The seeds you sew will lead to growth for those yet to be born. Embrace The Oneness. Ask when you need with an open heart, and receive what is right for you, others and 'The Way Of The Oneness.' Always "Walk in The Way of The Oneness." May The Oneness Force be with you always!

Note: Back in 1986, my saying was "Walk in the Way Of The Oneness." Now today I am known as "The Voice Of The Oneness." Please feel free to share this expression. "Walking in The Way Of The Oneness," brings a truly strong connection with all Fragments, on all Planes of Evolution, and their respective Levels too. Remember always to harmonize your Aura and the tune you play each day!

PRODUCTS & SERVICES
FROM SUMARIS ENTERPRISES

THERAPY KITS

Dr. Margaret's Crystal Acupuncture[sm] Therapy Kit

This amazing set contains 8 crystal points and 1 pendulum attractively packaged in a satin purse which can be easily carried in a handbag or pocket. Included in the kit is a Booklet of Crystal Acupuncture Diagrams. This clear and detailed work gives directions on the use of the points and pendulums and also presents valuable information on the Chakras, the Five Bodies, and the acupuncture meridians.

Dr. Margaret's Teragram[sm] Therapy Kit

Dispel the Madness with our kit containing one each of Natural, Blue, Violet, Red, Green and Pink Agate plates attractively contained in a satin drawstring pouch. A simple instruction booklet provides directions and tips. As a special bonus, we include a CD by Dr. Margaret Rogers Van Coops with a color meditation and a meditation for Chakra and Five Bodies balancing.

Dr. Margaret's "Core" Teragram[sm] Therapy Kit

Releases Negative History stored in your body's cells. Banishes effects of old issues. Strengthens you to deal with emotional and mental issues. Stimulates more efficient energy flow. Generates inner sense of well-being. Margaret Rogers Van Coops *"Core" Teragram[sm] Therapy Kit* contains 3 specially selected Agate slices with a Basic Relaxation Meditation CD featuring the nurturing voice of Dr. Stephen Van Coops. You will quickly enter into a deep alpha state ideal for releasing old emotional habits and irrelevant mind conditioning.

Dr. Margaret's spiritual Crystal Acupuncture[sm] Kit

Five triangular stones combined with four specially selected pointed stones to refine dense energy and to redirect it according to your desire or need. Kit includes detailed booklet with instructions and diagrams. spiritual Geometry leads to focus on spiritual reality beyond your previous physical awareness.

Dr. Margaret's TrinityStone[sm] Healing Kit

This unique kit allows auditory memory to stimulate and shift negativity from the body. the five specially selected large open equilateral triangles are used on the Chakras, one at a time, and Then all together to erase fear and illusions stored in associations with sounds. Each triangle, when added, will enhance your perception, vision, and positive sensations. Included is a booklet with instructions and diagrams and two isosceles triangles that are useful in raising the Kundalini and stimulating and harmonizing the Higher and Lower Sacred Centers. When all seven triangles are used together, an awakening may be realized that will result in an explosion of self-confidence.

Dr. Margaret's Facial Beauty Crystal Acupuncture[sm] Kit

Dr. Margaret's Beauty Crystal Acupuncture is an amazing way to lose your facial wrinkles and lines as well as to erase cellular memory from the many expressions you have made throughout your life. In this way this Therapy will remove both negative and emotional states long forgotten, thus allowing a rejuvenation of cells throughout your body.

BOOKS

The Rejection Syndrome

In our daily lives, all of us experience moments of rejection that create an internal impasse, either by ourselves or by others. My intent is to assist those wishing to be free of those encumbrances brought about by the **Rejection Syndrome**. This is about a pattern of existence that compounds habit, routine, and conditioning, leading to limitation, restriction, judgment, and competition. Learn about the *Soul Structure* and how you can use it to be aware of yourself and to perform to the best of your ability without negativity or rejection.

Pro-Life, Pro-Choice, Pro-Spirit

Spirit's truth is clearly shown through Margaret's own personal experiences. Is everything pre-ordained? the word "abortion" evokes emotions in almost all normally rational minds. Right or wrong? Moral or immoral? Should it be legal or illegal? One of the most burning issues of our time: Advocates of both sides have thrown Themselves at each other's faces even to the point of violence. This book is a must read for women who have been, are now or are likely to become pregnant. Without being judgmental, Dr. Margaret provides the wisdom of Master Teachers to assist women to acknowledge, accept and deal with their circumstances. She has crossed the worldly boundaries to discover just what really happens from the point of view of the child-to-be's spirit and spirit Master Teachers.

Discover Your Baby's Spirit

Every child is joined to a Mother before birth through the power of their individual *Soul Structures* and their earthly personalities. Dr. Margaret has produced an amazing book that will take the reader right into the heart of a Mother and her baby. the information is current and thought provoking and will help clarify why one chooses to be a Mother. At this time, the Hero, Star, Indigo, Crystal, and Liquid Crystal Children are being born. Dr.

Margaret shares how to avoid negative influences while caring for these enlightened children, as well as how to integrate a Mother 's lifestyle with that of her child from birth to adulthood. Discover who a child truly is, what their character and destiny might likely be, and get a glimpse of the wonderful reasons for sharing oneself as a Mother.

Breakthrough Therapies: Crystal Acupuncture^{sm} & Teragram^{sm} Therapy

While most people today vaguely realize that the body is a working machine that generates energy, most of us do not understand the way energy flows, where it goes, and what it does. ***Breakthrough Therapies*** is the product of Dr. Margaret's research with her clients and under medical supervision. Her research has validated the integration of the energies of the Five Bodies. The book reveals how the principles of Oriental Acupuncture, combined with the use of specially cut crystals and semi-precious stones, will unblock energy flow in our Five Bodies and will tone, stimulate, and balance the Chi energies. Using natural resonating energy stones and crystals such as, but not limited to Hematite, Jasper, Citrine, Amethyst, Carnelian and Quartz, has opened the door to drug-free, inexpensive solutions to emotional and psychological issues ranging from addictions to depression to stress. Dr. Margaret's powerful, non-invasive healing methods also provide remarkable relief from minor physical ailments like headaches to major illnesses and syndromes such as AIDS, Cancer and Multiple Sclerosis.

The Book of Crystal Acupuncture^{sm} & Teragram^{sm} Therapy Diagrams

Complementary Healing Therapy has taken another step forward with this amazing book illustrating and describing dozens of crystal stones and tools with techniques for effectively treating acute and chronic conditions suffered by humans and animals. From headaches and minor injuries to major complicated illnesses, Dr. Margaret's treatments provide effective non-invasive and inexpensive remedies to put you or your clients back into a state of positive healing. Dr. Margaret's work with her clients has further validated ancient Oriental Acupuncture principles and merged them with exciting, simple methods using crystals to unblock energy flow in your Five Bodies to tone, balance and stimulate your Chi energies. Her research has even carried this work into the treatment of pets and wildlife.

Journey into An Unknown World
The Way to Oneness Revisited

This inspiring work delves into the cosmology of multi-dimensional spiritual existence. Beginning with the "Word" as vibrational consciousness, this book takes you on a journey through the principles of creation, separation, the descending and ascending currents, faith, intuition, belief, and evolution. the various sub-divisional cosmologies of the seven archetypes and planes of existence are viewed. Also, incarnation, reincarnation and the Akashic Records are explained as an inter-relationship with the deep subconscious and the Chakras.

Of particularly unique interest is the principle of soul fragmentation that the book discusses throughout the text. *Journey into An Unknown World, the Way to Oneness Revisited* concludes with practical steps and techniques for emotional balancing and relaxation, disciplinary exercises, and various other psychic tools such as astrology, numerology, graphology, and palmistry. Spirit Guides Recommended for all practitioners seeking insight into higher knowledge. Included Channeled message from Master Guides between 1980-95 that have come to pass. — *James Ravenscroft, <u>Whole Life Times</u> March 15. 1990*

50 spiritually Powerful Meditations

In the stillness of the mind lies the answer to your purpose. Dr. Margaret has tested all of these meditations herself. By doing each of these meditations, you can find true direction for your life and release fears, pains, restrictions, and anger acquired through conditioning. These meditations work! Develop your psychic ability, fine tune your healing skills, mend relationships, empower yourself and much more. This should be a book on everyone's shelf.

Expanding Images With The OmniCard[sm]

This book fully explains the many aspects of the Psychic Abilities. Through understanding Psychometry, Clairvoyance, Clairaudience and Clairsentience (smell and Taste), with practice on the focus of images, sounds and feelings one can be guided to understand the way to develop these skills and to become a practicing psychic. This book also includes a simple collection of pictorial images of every part of the *OmniCard*[tm], where in-depth descriptions of the meanings of these symbols are explained.

The *OmniCard*[tm] is the simplest way of doing a psychic reading for yourself, your friends, or your clients. This revolutionary tool lets you easily tap into images that apply to questions being asked. This is a wonderful new adventure in learning and psychic awareness. Simply attune to a question and Then let your eyes scan the images until one looms up at you. Visualize the significance of the image and all the meanings it draws forth. It is like having an entire Tarot deck of cards in one stylistic full-color painting, evoking vivid, literal, and symbolic images. These images are the focal points for you to create a psychic reading that will entertain and amaze your friends and clients. There are many ways to interpret the answers to questions. Try experimenting with them and discover how effective you can be!

Henry's Secrets

In this gripping mystery, Dr. Margaret Rogers Van Coops, makes her debut into the world of fiction to explore human psyche. Meryl Jones, an African American single Mother has established herself in the world of advertising. Upon the death of her mentor, Henry Wiggins, she is plunged into a stream of events and revelations that turn her world upside down. The story careens into a surprising climax… a web of secrets spills out, changing everyone's lives forever…

Quantum Entanglement, A Paranormal Point of View

Maybe Albert Einstein's quote "If you can't explain it simply, you don't understand it well enough" attributed to this genius, is authentic or not, but the spirit of this book on the Theory of Quantum Entanglement is an enlightening example of complicated information presented in simple, easy to understand terms.

Dr. Margaret, like a seasoned tour leader, takes you on a journey of your mind, body, and spirit through the vast linked relationships among all forms of creation. From the quantum depths of the subatomic worlds to the endless reaches of intergalactic space, she binds you to all that is, in a comprehensive study of The Oneness and the interconnectedness of everything in it.

TrinityStone^{sm} Healing Therapy

Dr. Margaret's ground-breaking TrinityStone^{sm} Healing Therapy was originally inspired by her personal Spirit Guide, Master Chang, who, in his wisdom, knew that a great deal of everyone's energy was blocked by fears stemming from the various sounds made by the Earth and the animals on it. Most of us are unaware how vocal, mechanical, or energetic sounds reverberate and oscillate throughout the energies of the Five Bodies that make up our Aura.

In this book, she explains how sound can hurt or heal us. Her amazing insight into geometrical forms, especially triangles, has revolutionized healing. She explains how various cut equilateral and isosceles triangular stones can resolve conflict and establish harmony just by listening to a song or watching a movie or removing emotional and mental conditioning while in meditation. Her research has proven without doubt that the right sounds can heal each one of us.

My Journey Into The Oneness

From her British roots, Dr. Margaret's relationship with Spirit Guides has led her to become a skilled teacher and gifted psychic medium and has provided benefit to countless individuals around the world. This book will help you create your connection with **The Oneness**. Dr. Margaret shows how we are connected not only to our world, but also with the Spirit World and worlds beyond! Armed with the knowledge she shares here, you can embrace ways to live in harmony with people, animals, and the preservation of Earth and beyond. Dr. Margaret draws you into many intimate and exciting and bizarre experiences. This may also be your story! the most valuable thing you can learn about The Oneness in this story is that it could be a key to saving our society and our environment! Understanding **"The Oneness of All That Is"** will unite you with the Creator and lead you to appreciate the glory of His work. Find out here, how Dr. Margaret became… "The Voice of the Oneness."

The Dark Side

The information in this book will help you handle your connections with the Dark Side of Self. Dr. Margaret shows how we are connected not only to our world, but also with the Spirit World and worlds beyond. Armed with the knowledge she shares here, you can embrace ways to live in harmony with people, animals, and the preservation of Earth and beyond. Dr. Margaret draws you into many intimate and exciting and bizarre experiences. This may also be your story! the most valuable thing you can learn about the Dark Side in this book is that it could be a key to saving our society and our environment! Understanding the Dark Side will unite you with the Creator and lead you to appreciate the glory of His work.

The Light Side

In times long ago, before writing, Humans speculated about their lives and purpose. Today, we still wonder how we evolved and why we are surrounded with so many diverse circumstances. Earth is the Forth Plane of Evolution where The Dark & The Light combine in an ever-evolving lesson of emotional turmoil, where friction creates new forms. Learn how the Seven Planes of Evolution; their combined 49 Levels of Ascension and Descension allow Fragments to interact in various lives on Earth and within The Lower & Upper Astral where lessons are assimilated. Within The Oneness, energy is constantly rebalanced under the command of The Prime Fragment, we call God. In this book you will discover the amazing journeys that all Fragments must make from Dark to Light and return from Light to Dark in an ever evolving and expanding way that allows The Oneness to evolve. Understand how each Plane of Evolution has both unity and conflict occurring where many new creations are then mirror-imaged into human form. This Planet Earth is key to the survival of The Oneness.

REGENESIS – A Trilogy. Book 1: The Invasion

SUSAN HAMILTON embarks on a normal journey into London to visit her parents and winds up encountering violence and destruction on an unbelievable scale. Aliens have emitted an ultrasonic ray over London that reduces the local population to a basic level of survival; kill or be killed. Finding her parents dead, and meeting a policeman, Peter Knowls, they embark on a dangerous mission to stop the aliens from taking control of Earth and its species. As she fights her way across London, she encounters the aliens and learns to become telepathic, expanding her awareness and capabilities to fight back and save the world!

AUDIO CD's & MP3 Downloads & Oil Formula

Dr. Margaret Rogers Van Coops has given many informative and interesting lectures, which are available on audio. She also provides hypnosis and meditation CD's and MP3's for focus on specific problems, issues and conditions. Please contact Sumaris Education Center for titles and prices. Formulas or private hypnosis recording made per personal health issues and mailed upon request.

PERSONAL SERVICES

Dr. Margaret is available for private consultations and is also available to do recorded readings by mail or over the phone. Call: (928) 486-1893

Sumaris Center

321 Farallon Dr., Lake Havasu City, AZ 86403, USA.

www.sumariscenter.com

**For Questions or appointments email:
profmargaretrvc@gmail.com**

All Dr Margaret's softback books are available as e-books from www.amazon.com or www.easytimepublishing.com

Her on-line school courses set high standards that are available for you to study and receive certification and diplomas. www.easypeasysolutions.org

Or Join Her in her one on one or face to face groups at our Sumaris Education Center in Lake Havasu City or on www.zoom.com.

ABOUT THE AUTHOR

Dr. Margaret Rogers Van Coops has been an ordained minister and missionary of the Universal Christ Church (School of spiritualism) since 1983. She is currently the Pastor, Director of Education and Treasurer for UCC. Margaret is a professor with two Ph.D.'s, one specializing in Medical and Clinical Hypnotherapy and Behavioral Sciences, the other for her Paranormal/Alternative Medical research and teachings with her ground-breaking seven Crystal Therapies. Professor Margaret Rogers Van Coops, DCH(IM), has practiced successfully in Spain, France, Switzerland, India, Egypt, Japan, England, Mexico, Peru, and the United States. Her professional affiliations have included The Spiritualist Association of Great Britain, the British Astrological and Psychic Society, the International Medical and Dental Hypnosis Association, the International Association of Counselors and Therapists, the International Hypnosis Federation, the Professional Board of Hypnotherapy, and the American Counseling Association. Margaret was among the co-founders of the International Psychic Forum and the American Metaphysical Society. Her dynamic lectures and workshops in Japan and the U.S. have led to regular invitations as a keynote speaker and participant in international events, including Whole Life Expos and Lifeways/BMSE Expos in various American Cities and the Festivals for Mind, Body and Spirit in London, Boston, and Los Angeles. She is the author of seventeen metaphysically oriented texts and two novels. Her books have been published in Western and Eastern Europe as well as Germany, Russia, China, and India. Dr. Margaret has written screenplays including the *Regenesis Trilogy, Seeing Blind* and the *Survivor,* and she is negotiating production of several reality TV series treatments.

Dr. Margaret's TV series, Psychic Chit Chat, was aired weekly on many public access channels in Southern California and Arizona. The show featured Dr. Margaret and her husband, Dr. Stephen Van Coops, who passed into The Oneness on 20th December 2019. was also a Metaphysician and collaborator on her works. The couple discussed topical and controversial subjects from a metaphysical perspective.

Currently, she hosts Journey into An Unknown World, a Webtalk Radio Show, that has achieved high listenership and popularity. This educational **1/2 hr.** show addresses many of the topics featured in Psychic Chit Chat. You can listen to these shows from

www.webtalkradio.net/shows/journey-into-an-unknown-world/
or
Archived podcasts are available as free downloads
on iTunes: **https://itunes.apple.com/us/podcast/id383183988**

Also: www.youtube.com/user/drimargaret
&
Dr Margaret Speaks channel
www.sumariscenter.com
www.easypeasysolution.com
www.easypeasysolutions.com

For education & help contact
Prof. Margaret Rogers Van Coops:
profmargaretrvc@gmail.com

For products and session:
drmargaretrvc@gmail.com

Follow her on
LinkedIn, FB, Referral, twitter, Pinterest, Instagram

To invite Prof..Margaret to speak at your event or radio show
please contact:
JonPaul Fletcher: www.charmwishpr@gmail.com

www.ingramcontent.com/pod-product-compliance
Lightning Source LLC
Chambersburg PA
CBHW061526050726
47593CB00002B/685